Dickie Brennan's

PALACE café

THE FLAVOR *of* NEW ORLEANS

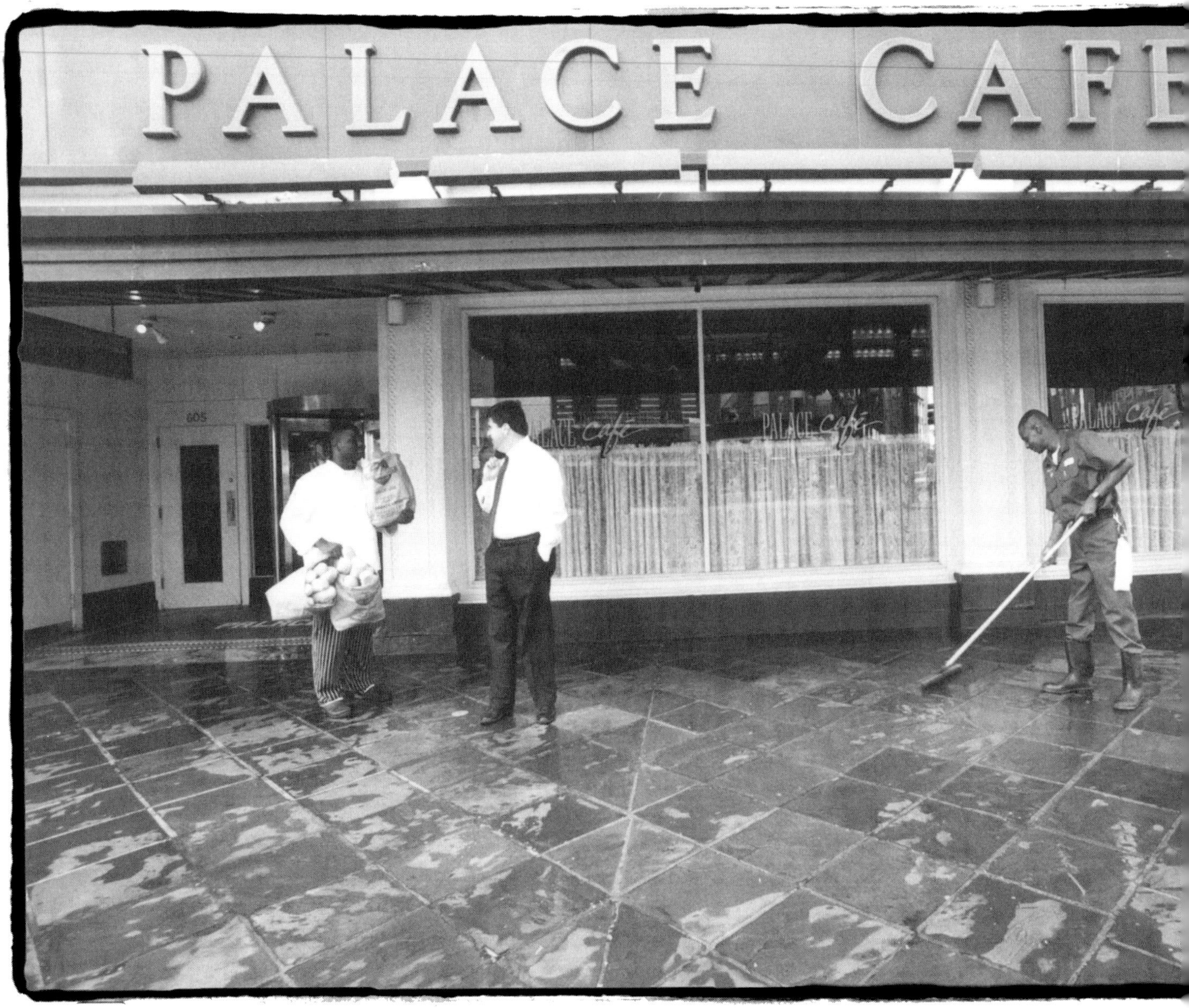
PALACE CAFE
605
PALACE Café
PALACE Café
PALACE Café

Dickie Brennan's

PALACE café

Dickie Brennan

with

Leslie Brennan and Gus Martin

Photography by
David Spielman

Food Photography
and
Cover Photograph by
Eugenia Uhl

THE FLAVOR *of* NEW ORLEANS

Palace Café
The Flavor of New Orleans

Published by Dickie Brennan & Co.
605 Canal Street
New Orleans, Louisiana 70130

Executive Editor: Leslie Brennan
Editorial Assistant: Emery Van Hook
Photography: David Spielman
        and Eugenia Uhl
Executive Chef: Gus Martin
Recipe Testing: Jeanette Martin and
        Linda Castanza
Contributors:
        Chef de Cuisine Darin Nesbit
        Pastry Chef Tobias Dotson
        Beverage Manager Jeff Gariss
        Bartender Mark Whalen
        Dr. Dale Edmonds

Edited, designed and manufactured
by Favorite Recipes® Press
an imprint of

FRP

2451 Atrium Way
Nashville, Tennessee 37214
1-800-358-0560

Art Director: Steve Newman
Book Design: Brad Whitfield
Production Design: Susan Breining
Project Manager: Jane Hinshaw
Project Production: Sara Anglin

ISBN: 1-931757-00-3
Manufactured in the United States
        of America
First Printing: 2002   15,000 copies

FOR DICK BRENNAN, FATHER AND MENTOR.
Your passion and love for family are examples for all to live by, and your sincere and genuine dedication to staff, customer and the business of hospitality has set a standard we hope to meet. Thank you for all you've given.

CONTENTS

MY FATHER TAUGHT US MANY THINGS IN THE COURSE

OF OUR GROWING-UP YEARS, AND ONE OF THE

GREATEST LESSONS HAS BEEN HIS BELIEF THAT OUR

RESTAURANTS ARE SIMPLY AN EXTENSION OF OUR OWN

HOME. THE NATURALNESS AND FLUIDITY EXUDED BY MY

DAD AS HE MOVED FROM KITCHEN TO DINING

ROOM WAS, AND IS, LIKE BEING HOME. "YOU TREAT THE

CUSTOMERS THE WAY YOU WOULD IF THEY WERE GUESTS

IN YOUR OWN HOME," HE STILL TELLS US REGULARLY.

"YOU TREAT THEM THE WAY YOU WANT TO BE TREATED."

INTRODUCTION

The Brennan family: (from left to right)
George Brower, Dick Brennan, Lindsey Brower, Brennan Brower, Lynne Brennan, Trist Brower, Lauren
Brennan Brower, Geordie Brower, Leslie Brennan, Richard Brennan, Sara Brennan and Dickie Brennan

I guess one might say that the restaurant business is in my blood, but, for me, I think it runs deeper than that. It runs through to my soul. It's a large part of who I am, and I've known it since I was ten years old. That's when I knew I wanted to work in the business.

Dickie Brennan

Despite the fact that I'm among the third generation of my restaurant family, I actually had a choice as to whether or not I wanted to make it my career. In fact, I'd go so far as to tell you that we—my twelve first cousins, my sister and I— were encouraged to look in other areas. And though some remain in other fields, eleven of us have found our way home to the restaurant business.

The Brennan family has been running restaurants since 1946. My dad, Dick Brennan, grew up in the kitchens of Brennan's Restaurant with his brothers, sisters and father, and moved over to Commander's Palace in 1974, where he remained until his "semi" retirement. Now, when he and Mom aren't taking advantage of some free time traveling, Dad can be found on any given day here at Palace Café, offering his wisdom and insight.

My sister Lauren, who can also be seen at Palace Café on a regular basis, and I grew up just blocks away from Commander's Palace. We spent our young lives working there in the kitchen, busing tables, or checking coats on a really busy night. Many days after school, I'd ride my bike to the restaurant and grab a snack of Veal Lafayette or whatever new dish the chef was working on, and so my craving for new tastes was born. Our father, Dick, encouraged Lauren and me to be around as much as we wanted, but he also pushed us to look at other careers that might interest us. He insisted on college degrees, and then we had to work outside of our restaurants for a while before he would consider our working permanently for the family.

The most valuable part of my education came after college when I worked in New York under the great chef Larry Forgioni and then in Paris at several of the grand cafés, such as Taillevent, La Tour

10

D'Argent and La Marée. The opportunity to see how things are done elsewhere was an invaluable experience. And, while wanting to implement many of the techniques and styles I picked up, I returned home with an even greater appreciation for our local resources and the talent that's in my own backyard.

By the time that I returned to the United States, Paul Prudhomme, an alumnus of Commander's Palace kitchen and a mentor to me, had been discovered by the rest of the world, not just by those of us in New Orleans. Emeril Lagasse had been given the lead in the kitchen at Commander's then and, again, was an inspiration to work with and a wonderful teacher to all those around him.

My Aunt Ella and Dad gave those of us who had decided to go into the business tremendous responsibilities in running and managing various aspects of the restaurants. This was a brave move on their part by any standard, but they let us get in and do it. "Use your judgment," they often directed. "What do you think?" I learned what it takes to run a restaurant by their example and through trial and error.

So, here we are today. But, I think it was inevitable. Passion for food and service that runs this deep isn't something you simply learn. As I said, I really think it's part of the genetic makeup. You can see it today, already, in some of our kids — I have two and my sister has four. Even now, they're begging to spend many of their summer days hanging out in the kitchen with the chefs. Their favorite is working with Pastry Chef Toby, making all sorts of grand and sweet creations, especially our family's originally-created Bananas Foster, flame and all . . . go figure.

It's also not uncommon to spot a member of the next generation working with the hostesses and seating people. Smiling politely and thanking customers for dining with us and wishing them a pleasant day or evening as they're leaving finishes out the customers' experience. The children know this, because it's what we, Lauren, our staff and I, do every day. It's because we're a family business, and we genuinely care about how your visit with us goes.

But our restaurant is about more than the Brennan family by far. It's about our extended family, our dedicated staff, the atmosphere of the restaurant itself and, of course, the culinary experience provided by our phenomenal talent in the kitchen under the guidance of Chef Gus Martin. Palace Café is about New Orleans. It's Southern hospitality in the grandest of traditions and fresh produce that springs forth from the rich soil of the Mississippi Delta and the waters of the Gulf of Mexico.

THE STYLE OF NEW ORLEANS

New Orleans, since its founding, has been a melting pot of European, Caribbean and African influences in culture and cuisine. It's the most difficult city to pin down by definition or description. But one thing is certain: It's full of life, richness and texture.

This city is steeped in various cultural traditions, which can also be seen in our architecture. Stepping into the French Quarter with its Italian, Spanish and French influences is, in many ways, like walking through a city in Europe. Palace Café is on Canal Street, the main downtown boulevard that's the door to the French Quarter, in a building that originated in 1901. Built for a gentleman named Phillip Werlein, who was in the music business, it's considered young in comparison to many of the surrounding buildings, particularly those farther into the heart of the Quarter.

One of our favorite historical "notes" about our building, if you will, is that it was the home of Werlein's for Music. The Werlein family has been in the music business for five generations now, longer than anyone else in America. Locally, this building is really well known, because musical greats such as Louis Armstrong, Fats Domino, Sweet Emma and Al Hirt

The Palace Café staircase

12

purchased their sheet music and supplies here. In honor of this heritage, we've kept the department listings in the elevator designating what was found on each floor of the old music store. And we pay tribute to New Orleans' musical sons and daughters in three huge murals in our second floor dining area.

It's here, in this old music building, that Palace Café was created. The center of the second floor was removed during construction to make room for a grand staircase. Visitors to the restaurant are taken up this staircase to the second floor dining room, where tables overlook the first floor and the boulevard. The intent was to make the restaurant look as though it had been in place for years, to complement the magnificence of the structure itself and the historical city in which it exists.

I grew up in a family where traditions are important. We honor our past and pay tribute to the future by preserving these historically valuable buildings. We can take what was old and make it fresh and new. Which brings us to our cuisine.

THE FLAVOR OF NEW ORLEANS

When we set out to define our style of cuisine at Palace Café, we couldn't narrow it down to a small restrictive label and so dubbed it "The Flavor of New Orleans." Fresh Creole and Cajun-influenced dishes are what we serve, with a touch of every country and culture that has made its historical mark on our city evident in our food. And yet, once you've tasted our style of cuisine, you'll be hard pressed to find anything anywhere with more flavor.

We've created many original dishes, but some of our dishes are traditional ones that have been re-created with something fresh and new to them. For example, red beans and rice is a Monday ritual for most New Orleanians. At Palace Café, we prepare it as a dip to be served with potato chips . . . delicious and fun. And, although cheesecake is usually a dessert, we make it with crabmeat and serve it as an appetizer.

Every day we start over, essentially, creating and re-creating, constantly striving to build, perfect, or even improve on what we're doing. It doesn't do just to sit back and watch. That's not the nature of this business or of anyone who feels the way we do about life. Just to spend a day around here would inspire anyone's creativity.

A restaurant day starts early. And, quite frankly, there's nothing in this world like watching the restaurant wake up. The streets are quiet, and the air is still damp from the night before. As the sun begins to warm things up, Chef Gus and his kitchen staff move through the morning routine of receiving the produce for the day and preparing what will be needed for that day's menu items. The aroma of freshly brewed coffee and chopped vegetables begins to take over, and the pace and rhythm of the day begins to pick up. Chef and his culinary crew move to the street just outside the Receiving Door of the restaurant to discuss the plans of the day, a tradition that now takes place before each meal service.

THE CHARACTER OF NEW ORLEANS

Familiar faces appear, as those who provide Palace Café with our ingredients pull up to the Receiving Door. We know each other's children and families. And, as Sal Sunseri, whose family at P & J Oysters has been selling to us for over fifty years now, drops the last sack of oysters at the Receiving Door, we're sure to ask about his son.

Louisiana blue crabs, crawfish and jumbo shrimp have been delivered by the same folks at Christina Seafood since the day we opened the doors to Palace Café more than ten years ago and, before that, to my parents' restaurants. I can say the same thing about the guy who brings us the fresh tuna from New Orleans Fish House.

I once had a conversation with Rose over at Christina Seafood, who told me she knew from memory exactly what each of her chefs wants. She calls the second it's available to set up the delivery. And Ted Kennedy, well, he and I went to high school together. He started City Herb. So when he makes an herb delivery, we usually share a laugh and check in on the status of our sons' baseball team because they're the same age.

Pecans from Bergeron Pecans in New Roads, Louisiana, are delivered regularly because we try to use them whenever we put nuts in a recipe. Why? Because we don't grow any other nut in this region, and it doesn't represent who we are as well to cook with almonds or walnuts. But, John Perrone over at Progress Grocery is sure to let us know when he's gotten something in fresh that may not be indigenous to our region, and we'll run it as a special. And Betty Landry, who grows blueberries for us in Poplarville, Mississippi, is a big hit by midsummer. Crates of the freshest, fattest blueberries you've ever seen go into making great salads, fresh fruit beignets, and many other desserts.

My friend Sandy Whann, whose family has been selling us our French bread for eons, is a bread fanatic. I trust his product from Leidenheimer the same way I trust my cream from Brown's Velvet Dairy and all the other purveyors mentioned. We see all these people constantly, and not just through business. Our friendships have been cultivated for a long time, now, and we trust one another. Their reputation, and ours, rides on the assurance that we receive and provide the best.

So when it comes to our White Chocolate Bread Pudding, we send all the way to Switzerland for the white chocolate. It's the quality that counts, and it has paid off. In the first ten years that Palace Café was open, we used thirty-four tons of white chocolate. We still look at one another wondering whether or not that can actually be true . . . but it is.

We believe that Palace Café is only as good as the product we start out with. This is why we've listed the products that we use in our recipes, along with suggested substitutions in some cases. But do some experimenting with what's available to you locally. Fresh regional products can't be improved upon, but just in case you're interested, we've listed sources for the exact ingredients that we use here. Remember, it's all about flavor and, depending on the ingredients you use, the flavor of the dish changes.

My family and I invite you to enjoy the many creations within this book.

And should your travels bring you to our hometown, please say hello and let us know what some of your favorite recipes are. Or, if you're like some of our friends and are just in the mood to be pampered and taken care of, by all means, we'll be glad to do just that. We promise a meal you'll never forget. . . after all, this is the *Flavor of New Orleans* that we're so famous for.

I speak for the entire staff at Palace Café, my sister Lauren and my family when I say that I hope this book brings you as much pleasure cooking at home as cooking brings us here. And if a recipe stirs some creative urge in you, moving you to make the dish more personally yours, then remember: that's the stuff great chefs are made of, whether at home or in the restaurant.

Lauren Brennan Brower and Dickie Brennan

ACKNOWLEDGEMENTS

Opening Palace Café was a dream of mine for years before it ever came into being. Maybe not this location specifically, or the precise twist of the massive staircase, but in my vision, I saw an old building and a grand staircase much like the ones in the grand cafés where I worked in Paris earlier in my life. Beyond the vision, there's no way I can take total credit for this becoming a reality. I threw out the idea, and it caught fire with several people who seem to share my love of the restaurant business.

I attribute much of where I am today to a strong family that sent me out into the world well equipped. My dad, Dick Brennan, has shared so much about the restaurant business with me and my sister throughout our lives. His love of travel and for the city of Paris and its cuisine gave a broader perspective and greater appreciation for what could be achieved.

16

To this day, Lynne Brennan, my mom, urges and supports us to grow and move forward. She never allowed us to feel that anything was unattainable, but insisted that hard work and a belief in oneself is all that's required for success. When confronted with a challenge, her response has always been, "Why not?"

Everyone needs a cheerleader—someone who's always there to support and encourage you. My sister, Lauren, has been that for me since we were small, so when I finally realized that Palace Café was to become a reality, Lauren quickly joined ranks. She left her position at Commander's Palace and has been a constant at Palace Café ever since. I appreciate her insight and dedication to family and the business. It's wonderful to have her as a business partner.

I'm eternally thankful for my business partner Steve Pettus. He was working for a hotel in New Orleans while I was working

Dickie Brennan, business partner Steve Pettus and Executive Chef Gus Martin

at Commander's Palace in 1990 and setting up the opening team for the Palace. He fell in love with the project and, within a short while, was matching my work schedule. He's now a partner in Dickie Brennan's Steakhouse and Bourbon House, our seafood restaurant. He's the quintessential partner, holding fast to the same standards and values my family has lived by for three generations.

Creating this book has been a blessing. It's hard to imagine the amount of work and attention to detail that goes into a book of this sort—a project that could never have been done without the help of so many people. The commitment shown to the project has been an inspiration, and the willingness and enthusiasm shared by all who participated have brought the idea of "team concept" to a new level.

There's no way to acknowledge individually each of our waitstaff, managers, administrators and culinary crew, but they are the best. Day in and day out, they make it possible to bring our interpretation of New Orleans dining to our guests. They *are* Palace Café.

Thanks must go to Executive Chef Gus Martin for his constant gift of creating fabulous food. He's been with my family since he was sixteen years old and is one of the most talented chefs I've ever worked with. He and his incredible kitchen staff, particularly Pastry Chef Tobias Dotson and Chef de Cuisine Darin Nesbit, did a wonderful job with the recipes for this book.

Executive Chef Gus Martin

Bartender Mark Whalen

Mark Whalen, who's been behind the bar since we opened our doors more than ten years ago, is the ultimate bartender and was fabulous in translating what he does every day into the beverage recipes. Our team captain, General Manager Mike Cobb, has been great throughout this process, helping to pull the whole thing together while keeping the restaurant running at a smooth pace.

A major contributor to this book, Emery Van Hook, came to our team as a college intern and is now a Marketing Manager.

Her attention to detail in working with the culinary staff and the recipes, organizing and scheduling the test kitchen and the countless other tasks, speak to her talents and abilities, which we recognized early on. The hours spent researching history, foods, sources and resources make this book what it is. She was invaluable to this project and made it all work.

Finally, an incredible amount of thanks must go to Leslie Brennan, my wife, who has translated my vision of Palace Café and my love for what I do into words. She's been a constant source of inspiration throughout the creative process and the driving force behind this project. Without her, this book wouldn't have been possible. Thank you, Leslie, for sharing your talents with all of us and for sharing your life with me.

General Manager Michael Cobb and members of the waitstaff

Leslie Brennan and Emery Van Hook

Dickie Brennan

19

BEVERAGES □

B R U N C H ▫ B R E A D

THERE'S NOTHING QUITE LIKE WATCHING THE RESTAURANT WAKE UP.

THE STREETS ARE QUIET, AND THE AIR IS STILL DAMP FROM THE NIGHT

BEFORE. AS CHEF GUS AND HIS KITCHEN STAFF BEGIN TO MOVE

THROUGH THE MORNING ROUTINE OF RECEIVING THE PRODUCE FOR

THE DAY, THE WAITSTAFF GATHERS FOR "PRE-MEAL" TO HEAR WHAT

CREATIONS THEY WILL HAVE TO OFFER. THE DAY'S MENU MOVES

FROM CREATIVE THOUGHT TO EXECUTION.

JAZZ BRUNCH AT THE NATCHEZ EOLA HOTEL

Natchez, Mississippi

Natchez is a popular tourist destination, known for its magnificent

old plantation homes. The newly refurbished Natchez Eola Hotel invited

Palace Café and Dickie Brennan to prepare a brunch in the

summer of 1992 for its River Road Food Festival.

MENU

Creole Onion Soup

Eggs Eola

White Chocolate Bread Pudding

NAPA VALLEY WINE AUCTION DINNER

Napa Valley, California

The Napa Valley Wine Auction is one of the largest nonprofit fundraisers in the country, raising millions of dollars every year to support its area hospitals. Guest chefs are invited to participate. In 1993, Dickie Brennan, along with other New Orleanian chefs Frank Brigtsen, Paul Prudhomme and Susan Spicer, was invited to participate in a seated dinner for 1600 guests on the eve of the auction. The menu is a combination of the chefs' creativity, with Palace Café preparing the appetizer and the dessert course.

MENU

Crawfish Sauté
with Popcorn Rice Cakes

Spinach Salad with Andouille Vinaigrette and Spiced Pecans

Grilled Duck Breast with Cracklin Cornbread,
Pickled Red Onions and Orange-Honey Creole Mustard Sauce

White Chocolate Bread Pudding

HURRICANES

INGREDIENTS

1 3/4 cups light rum
1 1/4 cups dark rum
1 1/2 cups freshly squeezed
   orange juice
1 1/2 cups pineapple juice
1/2 cup cranberry juice
1/2 cup sour mix
2 tablespoons grenadine

GARNISH

orange slices
maraschino cherries

■ *Makes 1 1/2 quarts*

Combine the light rum, dark rum, orange juice, pineapple juice, cranberry juice, sour mix and grenadine in a large pitcher or shaker and mix well. Serve over ice in glasses and garnish with orange slices and maraschino cherries.

BLOODY MARYS

INGREDIENTS

1 cup Worcestershire sauce
1/2 cup beef broth
2 tablespoons Rose's lime juice
10 dashes of Tabasco hot sauce
1 tablespoon (heaping) prepared
   horseradish (optional)
1 tablespoon (heaping) celery salt
1 tablespoon (heaping) white pepper
2 (46-ounce) cans tomato juice
vodka to taste

GARNISH

lemon and lime wedges
olives
spiced green beans

■ *Makes 1 gallon*

Combine the Worcestershire sauce, beef broth, lime juice, hot sauce, horseradish, celery salt and white pepper in a large pitcher or shaker. Shake or stir until the celery salt dissolves. Add the tomato juice and mix well. Chill, covered, in the refrigerator for 8 hours or longer if possible to blend the flavors.

Add the vodka just before serving. Serve over ice in tall glasses. Garnish with lemon and lime wedges, olives and spiced green beans.

For Creole Bloody Marys, follow the recipe for Bloody Marys, substituting pepper-flavored vodka for the plain vodka.

RAMOS GIN FIZZ

INGREDIENTS

1 egg white
1/4 cup half-and-half
3/4 cup sour mix
1/2 ounce simple syrup
1/3 ounce Rose's lime juice
1 1/2 ounces gin
splash of soda water
2 small drops of orange flower water

■ *Serves 1*

Combine the egg white, half-and-half, sour mix, simple syrup, lime juice and gin in a glass or blender and mix until smooth or blend at medium-low speed for 10 seconds or until smooth. Pour over ice to chill and strain into a rocks glass. Top with soda water and add the orange flower water.

MILK PUNCH

INGREDIENTS

4 cups milk
1 cup brandy or bourbon
1/4 cup vanilla extract
1/4 cup simple syrup
1 pint vanilla ice cream

GARNISH

nutmeg

■ *Makes 1 1/2 quarts*

Photograph for this recipe is on page 45.

Combine the milk, brandy, vanilla, simple syrup and ice cream. Blend for 8 seconds. Garnish with a sprinkle of nutmeg.

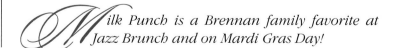

Milk Punch is a Brennan family favorite at Jazz Brunch and on Mardi Gras Day!

DICKIE BRENNAN'S FRUIT PUNCH

INGREDIENTS

1 ounce (2 tablespoons) citron-flavored vodka
1/2 ounce (1 tablespoon) peach schnapps
1/2 ounce (1 tablespoon) coconut-flavored rum
pineapple juice
cranberry juice
soda water

GARNISH

orange slice
maraschino cherry

■ *Serves 1*

Combine the vodka, schnapps and rum over ice in a tall glass. Add equal parts of pineapple juice and cranberry juice and mix gently. Finish with a splash of soda water and garnish with an orange slice and a maraschino cherry.

ABSINTHE SUISSESSE

INGREDIENTS

11/2 ounces (3 tablespoons) Herbsaint
1/2 ounce (1 tablespoon) orgeat syrup
1 egg white
1 teaspoon white crème de menthe

■ *Serves 1*

Place 4 ounces of ice in a blender and add the Herbsaint, orgeat syrup, egg white and white crème de menthe. Blend at low speed for 8 seconds. Pour into a chilled rocks glass.

Herbsaint is an anise-flavored liqueur that is New Orleans' version of pastis, a lighter relative of absinthe. Several herbs, in addition to the anise, give the liqueur a complex flavor. Other anise liqueurs can be substituted where Herbsaint isn't available.

Orgeat syrup is made from almonds, sugar and rose water or orange flower water. It can be hard to find, but stores that handle coffee syrups or flavoring sometimes carry it. Almond syrup is an acceptable substitution.

HARRY'S BELLINI

INGREDIENTS

1/4 Champagne glass white peach
    nectar, chilled
dash of peach schnapps
3/4 glass Champagne, chilled

■ *Serves 1*

Pour the peach nectar into a Champagne glass. Add a dash of peach schnapps and finish with the Champagne.

MINT JULEP

INGREDIENTS

8 fresh mint leaves
1 tablespoon simple syrup
2 ounces (1/4 cup) bourbon

GARNISH

1 whole sprig of mint

■ *Serves 1*

Tear the mint leaves into tiny pieces in a tall glass, discarding the stems. Cover with the simple syrup and muddle the mixture with the back of a spoon for 10 seconds. Fill the glass with crushed ice and add the bourbon. Garnish with a mint sprig.

Mint Julep is a southern classic. The secret of a good mint julep is to tear the leaves into very fine pieces in order to release and intensify the aroma and flavor of the mint.

Pimm's Cup

Ingredients

2 ounces (1/4 cup) Pimm's
3 ounces (6 tablespoons) sour mix
soda water

Garnish

chilled cucumber stick

■ *Serves 1*

Pour the Pimm's and sour mix over ice in a tall glass. Fill the glass with soda water and garnish with a cucumber stick.

Sazerac

Ingredients

2¹/2 ounces (5 tablespoons)
    rye whiskey
1 teaspoon simple syrup
3 dashes of Angostura bitters
3 dashes of Peychaud bitters
dash of Herbsaint (see Note
    page 26)

Garnish

lemon twist

■ *Serves 1*

Combine the rye whiskey, simple syrup and bitters over ice in a container and stir to mix well. Swirl the Herbsaint in a rocks glass to coat it well and pour out the excess. Strain the whiskey mixture into the prepared glass and garnish with a lemon twist.

The Sazerac is named for the Sazerac Coffee House in New Orleans where it was first served.

EGGS CHARTRES

CHORON SAUCE

2 tomatoes, coarsely chopped
1 dried shallot, chopped
1/2 cup red wine
1 tablespoon rice wine vinegar
2 teaspoons fresh or dried tarragon
5 egg yolks
1 teaspoon Tabasco sauce
1 teaspoon lemon juice
2 tablespoons water
1 pound butter, clarified
    (see Note page 31)
kosher salt and white pepper to taste

EGGS

tops of 2 green onions
4 cups water
1/2 cup white vinegar
8 eggs
4 slices Brioche (page 47)
4 mushroom sausage links or
    patties, or other sausage
    (page 78)

■ *Serves 4*

FOR THE SAUCE, cook the tomatoes with the shallot, red wine, wine vinegar and tarragon in a saucepan over medium heat until most of the liquid is evaporated. Cool to room temperature.

Whisk the egg yolks, Tabasco sauce, lemon juice and water in a double boiler or metal bowl atop a saucepan of boiling water. Cook until the mixture is almost triple the original volume and pale yellow, whisking rapidly; remove from the heat during the cooking period if necessary to prevent the eggs from scrambling.

Remove from the heat and whisk in the clarified butter gradually until thick and creamy. Stir in the tomato reduction and season with kosher salt and white pepper. Keep warm.

FOR THE EGGS, slice the green onion tops thinly lengthwise and place in a bowl of ice water to curl. Preheat the oven to 350 degrees.

Bring 4 cups of water to a boil in a large saucepot. Stir in the vinegar. Break the eggs carefully into the water in batches if necessary to prevent crowding. Poach for 3 minutes or until done to taste. Remove to a skillet of warm water and keep warm.

Cut each slice of brioche diagonally into halves and place on a baking sheet. Toast lightly in the preheated oven. Slice the sausage links lengthwise. Grill the sausage over hot coals or sauté in a sauté pan until brown.

To assemble, remove the green onion curls from the water and gently pat dry. Place 2 pieces of brioche on each serving plate. Remove the eggs from the water with a slotted spoon and drain well, blotting with a paper towel to remove the excess water. Trim the edges if necessary. Place 1 egg on each piece of brioche and top with the desired amount of Choron Sauce. Top with the green onion curls and serve with the sausage.

This dish is named for Chartres Street, which begins at Palace Café's receiving door and ends at Jackson Square, the heart of the French Quarter.

SHRIMP SCRAMBLED EGGS IN PUFF PASTRY WITH ANDOUILLE CREAM

ANDOUILLE CREAM

8 ounces andouille sausage
2 tablespoons butter
1 tablespoon chopped garlic
1/2 cup chopped red onion
2 tablespoons bourbon
4 cups heavy cream
kosher salt and cracked black
    pepper to taste

SHRIMP SCRAMBLED EGGS

4 frozen puff pastry squares, thawed
12 eggs
kosher salt and cracked black
    pepper to taste
1/4 cup (1/2 stick) butter
12 ounces (36- to 40-count) shrimp,
    peeled, deveined, chopped
1/4 cup thinly sliced green onion tops

■ *Serves 4*

FOR THE ANDOUILLE CREAM, grind the sausage coarsely in a food processor. Melt the butter in a sauté pan and add the garlic. Sauté until golden brown. Add the onion and sauté until tender. Add the sausage and cook, covered, over medium heat for 15 to 20 minutes or until cooked through.

Add the bourbon, stirring to deglaze the sauté pan. Add the cream and cook over high heat for 20 to 30 minutes or until the sauce thickens enough to coat the spoon, stirring occasionally. Season with kosher salt and pepper.

FOR THE EGGS, preheat the oven to 375 degrees. Place the pastry on a baking sheet and bake for 15 to 20 minutes or until puffed and golden brown. Whisk the eggs with kosher salt and pepper to taste in a large mixing bowl.

Preheat a large nonstick omelette or sauté pan and melt the butter in it. Add the shrimp and sauté until partially cooked. Add the eggs and cook just until the eggs are soft-set and the shrimp are cooked through.

To serve, split the pastry squares horizontally. Spoon andouille cream onto 4 serving plates and place the bottom halves of the pastry squares in the center of each plate. Spoon the egg mixture onto the pastry squares and top with the remaining pastry. Sprinkle with the green onion tops.

BACON AND PORT SALUT OMELETTE
WITH PARSLEY POTATOES

PARSLEY POTATOES

4 cups vegetable oil for frying
1 pound Idaho potatoes, about
    2 large potatoes, chopped into
    1/4-inch pieces
1/2 teaspoon chopped garlic
2 tablespoons butter
1 teaspoon chopped parsley
1 teaspoon Creole seasoning

OMELETTE

6 ounces bacon, chopped
1 tablespoon butter
1/2 cup julienned onion
4 ounces mushrooms, sliced
1 tablespoon clarified butter
12 eggs
1/4 teaspoon salt
1/8 teaspoon cracked black pepper
4 ounces Port Salut cheese,
    shredded, or cut into 1/2-inch
    pieces
tops of 2 green onions, chopped

■ *Serves 4*

FOR THE POTATOES, preheat the vegetable oil to 350 degrees in a deep fryer or large saucepan. Blanch the potatoes in a saucepan of boiling water and remove to a bowl of cold water to stop the cooking process; drain. Fry the drained potatoes in the oil until golden brown and remove with a slotted spoon to paper towels to drain.

Sauté the garlic in the butter in a large sauté pan until golden brown. Add the potatoes and sauté over medium heat for about 2 minutes. Stir in the parsley and season with Creole seasoning. Keep warm.

FOR THE OMELETTE, partially cook the bacon in a small skillet. Melt 1 tablespoon butter in a sauté pan and add the onion. Sauté until the onion begins to caramelize; remove from the heat.

Preheat a nonstick omelette pan over medium heat and add the partially cooked bacon. Sauté until crisp. Add the mushrooms, caramelized onions and clarified butter. Sauté until the mushrooms are tender; remove from the heat. Whisk the eggs, salt and pepper in a mixing bowl.

Spoon 1/4 of the bacon, onion and mushrooms into the omelette pan for each omelette and spread evenly. Pour in 1/4 of the egg mixture. Scramble lightly with a wooden spoon or rubber spatula, moving the pan and the spoon at the same time until the eggs begin to set. Add 1/4 of the cheese and cook until the eggs are set without stirring.

Roll the omelettes onto serving plates with a rubber spatula and sprinkle with chopped green onion tops. Serve with the Parsley Potatoes.

The trick to making omelettes is to use a good, coated nonstick omelette pan. If you find rolling the omelette difficult, try making a frittata. Cook the eggs completely in the omelette pan over low heat and then transfer the flat round frittata to a serving plate with a spatula.

To clarify butter, melt unsalted butter in a saucepan over low heat, skimming and discarding any foam from the surface. Spoon or pour the clear golden butter carefully off the milk solids, which will settle to the bottom.

CAFÉ EGGS BENEDICT

PORK DEBRIS

1 (5- to 7-pound) Boston pork butt
kosher salt and cracked black
    pepper or Creole seasoning
    to taste
8 cups (about) chicken stock
    (page 197) or canned
    chicken broth
1 cup roasted garlic

SWEET CHEDDAR CHEESE BISCUITS

3 cups all-purpose flour
1 cup cake flour
1/2 cup sugar
2 tablespoons baking powder
1/4 teaspoon salt
1/2 cup (1 stick) butter, chilled, sliced
1 1/2 cups freshly grated mild
    Cheddar cheese
1 1/2 cups buttermilk

POACHED EGGS

3 cups water
1/2 cup white vinegar
24 eggs
Hollandaise Sauce (page 193)

■ *Serves 12*

FOR THE PORK DEBRIS, season the Boston butt on all sides with salt and pepper or Creole seasoning and place in a large baking dish. Roast, uncovered, at 350 degrees for 45 to 55 minutes. Add enough chicken stock to fill the baking dish half full. Cover with foil and roast for 1 hour. Add the roasted garlic and roast for 30 minutes longer or until the pork is falling from the bone.

Remove from the oven and cool to room temperature. Pull the pork from the bone with a fork, discarding the skin and bone.

FOR THE BISCUITS, preheat the oven to 350 degrees. Combine the all-purpose flour, cake flour, sugar, baking powder and salt in a medium mixing bowl. Cut in the butter with two knives or a pastry cutter until the mixture is in crumbs the size of small peas. Mix in the cheese. Add the buttermilk and mix into a slightly wet and sticky dough with your hands; do not overmix.

Place dough on a work surface lightly sprinkled with flour and sprinkle the top lightly with additional flour. Knead lightly and pat or roll 1 inch thick. Cut into 3-inch circles with a cutter dipped in flour, starting at the edge closest to you and cutting clockwise; cut the center last. Place on a baking sheet lined with parchment or sprayed with nonstick baking spray. Bake for 30 minutes or until golden brown.

FOR THE EGGS, bring the water and vinegar to a boil in a large saucepan. Add the eggs carefully and poach until done to taste.

To serve, split the biscuits into halves horizontally. Place both halves cut side up on each serving plate and top with a generous helping of the pork. Place a poached egg on each biscuit and spoon Hollandaise Sauce over the eggs.

There are many ways to prepare Eggs Benedict. This is Palace Café's version of the classic dish. By "debris," we mean meat cooked so tender, it literally falls off the bone.

EGGS EOLA

INGREDIENTS

6 tablespoons (3/4 stick)
   unsalted butter
4 boneless skinless chicken breasts
8 garlic cloves, minced
2 cups chopped boiled ham
12 fresh mushrooms, chopped
16 green onion tops, coarsely
   chopped
6 tablespoons (3/4 stick)
   unsalted butter
1/4 cup dry white wine
vegetable oil for frying
2 cups finely chopped potatoes
salt and pepper to taste
8 poached eggs
Béarnaise Sauce (page 192)

■ *Serves 4*

Preheat the oven to 400 degrees. Melt 6 tablespoons butter in a shallow baking pan. Place the chicken in the butter, turning to coat well and arranging in the pan. Bake for 10 to 15 minutes or until light brown and cooked through; keep warm.

Sauté the garlic, ham, mushrooms and green onion tops in 6 tablespoons butter in a large sauté pan until tender-crisp. Add the wine and simmer until the liquid is slightly reduced.

Heat the vegetable oil to 350 degrees in a deep skillet or deep fryer. Fry the potatoes until crisp and golden brown. Remove with a slotted spoon to drain on paper towels. Add the potatoes to the vegetable and wine mixture and toss lightly. Season with salt and pepper.

To serve, spoon the potato mixture onto serving plates. Shred the chicken over the potato mixture. Top each portion with 2 poached eggs and 2 tablespoons Béarnaise Sauce.

Eggs Eola was served at The Natchez Eola Hotel for the Second Annual River Road Food Festival. The hotel, built in 1927, is an Historic Hotel of America as designated by the National Trust for Historic Preservation.

PAN HASH AND EGGS

INGREDIENTS

8 ounces pickled pork
vegetable oil for frying
2 cups chopped Idaho potatoes
1/2 cup (1 stick) butter
2 teaspoons chopped garlic
1 cup half-moon sliced leeks
1 cup mixed chopped green, red
    and yellow bell peppers
Creole seasoning to taste
8 eggs
8 slices bacon, crisp-fried
1/2 cup chopped green onion tops

■ *Serves 4*

Bring a small saucepan of water to a boil and add the pickled pork. Cook until the pork is tender. Let stand until cool enough to handle then chop.

Heat the vegetable oil to 350 degrees in a large skillet or saucepan. Add the potatoes and fry until crisp and golden brown; drain on paper towels.

Melt the butter in a cast-iron skillet and add the garlic. Sauté until golden brown. Add the leeks, bell peppers and pickled pork. Sauté until the vegetables are tender-crisp. Stir in the fried potatoes and season with Creole seasoning. Keep warm over low heat.

Preheat an omelette pan sprayed with nonstick cooking spray over medium heat. Break the eggs into the pan and cook sunny side up until done to taste.

To serve, spoon the hash onto serving plates and place 2 eggs on the hash on each plate. Crisscross 2 slices of bacon over the eggs and sprinkle with the chopped green onion tops.

If you can't find or don't like pickled pork, try substituting chopped tasso, ham or a spicy sausage. The hash will have a different flavor depending on what you use, but it tastes great with any of these. You might also try using apple-smoked bacon for added flavor. In the restaurant, we serve our Pan Hash and Eggs in individual French pans.

LYONNAISE GULF FISH WITH POACHED EGGS

LEMON BEURRE BLANC WITH CARAMELIZED ONIONS

3 whole lemons, peeled
1 shallot, chopped
2 bay leaves
4 black peppercorns
1/2 cup white wine
1/2 cup heavy whipping cream
2 cups (4 sticks) butter, chopped, chilled
1 large yellow onion, julienned
1/2 cup (1 stick) butter
kosher salt and white pepper to taste

LYONNAISE GULF FISH

4 Idaho potatoes, peeled, grated or shredded
3 eggs
1 cup milk
2 cups all-purpose flour
2 tablespoons Creole seasoning
8 (3-ounce) white fish fillets
kosher salt and cracked black pepper or Creole seasoning to taste
1 1/2 cups vegetable oil for frying
3 cups water
1/2 cup white vinegar
8 eggs
Choron Sauce (page 193)
chopped fresh chives

■ *Serves 4*

FOR THE BEURRE BLANC, combine the lemons, shallot, bay leaves, peppercorns and wine in a medium saucepan and cook over medium-high heat until reduced by 1/2. Whisk in the heavy cream and cook until thickened, stirring occasionally.

Reduce the heat to low and add 2 cups chilled butter 1 piece at a time, whisking constantly to incorporate before adding more butter; the sauce will break if the butter is added too quickly. Remove from the heat and pour through a fine strainer into a clean saucepan.

Sauté the onion in 1/2 cup butter in a skillet until well caramelized. Add to the strained sauce and season to taste.

FOR THE FISH, combine the grated or shredded potatoes with water to cover in a bowl to prevent darkening. Beat 3 eggs with the milk in a shallow dish. Mix the flour with 2 tablespoons Creole seasoning.

Season the fish on both sides with kosher salt and cracked pepper or Creole seasoning. Dip into the egg mixture and dust with the seasoned flour, shaking off the excess.

Drain the grated potato well and press over both sides of the fish fillets. Heat the oil in a large skillet until hot but not smoking. Add the fish carefully and cook for 4 to 5 minutes on each side or until golden brown; drain well. Place on an ovenproof platter and place in a warm oven until ready to serve. Bring the water and vinegar to a simmer in a large saucepan. Break the 8 eggs into the saucepan in batches if necessary to prevent crowding. Poach for 3 minutes or until done to taste.

To serve, ladle the Lemon Beurre Blanc onto 4 serving plates. Place a fish fillet on each prepared plate and top with two poached eggs. Drizzle with Choron Sauce and sprinkle with chives.

Seafood Crêpes

Mushroom Cream Sauce

2 cups heavy whipping cream
1 cup sliced leeks
2 cups sliced mixed wild mushrooms, such as shiitake, crimini, chanterelle, oyster or button
1 tablespoon butter
kosher salt and white pepper

Filled Crêpes

1 teaspoon chopped garlic
1 tablespoon butter
4 ounces (36- to 40-count) shrimp, peeled, chopped
4 ounces crawfish tails (optional)
1/2 cup mixed chopped green, red and yellow bell peppers
1/2 cup chopped yellow onion
1/2 cup sliced green onions
4 ounces jumbo lump crabmeat
1 pint oysters (optional)
2 tablespoons chopped fresh thyme
6 ounces cream cheese, softened
Creole seasoning to taste
Crêpes (page 37)

Garnish

shaved truffle cheese

■ *Serves 8*

For the cream sauce, cook the cream in a heavy saucepot over medium-high heat until reduced by 1/2, stirring occasionally with a wooden spoon. Sauté the leeks and mushrooms in the butter in a large sauté pan. Add to the cream. Cook until the mixture is thickened enough to coat the back of a spoon. Season with kosher salt and white pepper. Cover and keep warm.

For the filled crêpes, sauté the garlic in the butter in a sauté pan until golden brown. Add the shrimp, crawfish tails, bell peppers, onion and green onions. Sauté until the seafood is almost fully cooked and the vegetables are tender-crisp.

Add the crabmeat and oysters and cook for 3 to 5 minutes longer. Remove from the heat and fold in the thyme and cream cheese. Season with Creole seasoning. Allow to cool while the crêpes are prepared.

To serve, spoon about 2 tablespoons of the cooled filling into the center of each crêpe and roll to enclose the filling. Arrange in a baking dish and heat in a 350-degree oven for 5 to 7 minutes or until heated through. Remove to serving plates and spoon warm cream sauce over the top. Garnish with shaved truffle cheese.

You may also sauté the filled crêpes in a small amount of butter in a sauté pan until heated through if preferred.

We love this dish finished with shaved truffle cheese, but it can be difficult to find and expensive. Gruyère cheese is a good substitute. You may substitute oysters for the crawfish tails in the filling, or use both if you like. If you have extra time, toss the sliced mushrooms with a little vegetable oil, kosher salt and cracked pepper and roast at 350 degrees for 10 to 12 minutes instead of sautéing them.

CRÊPES

^{1}/2 cup all-purpose flour
^{1}/2 cup milk
^{1}/4 cup water
2 eggs
2 tablespoons butter, melted
1 cup mixed chopped herbs, such as
    oregano, thyme, basil and chives
    (optional)
pinch of salt

FOR THE CRÊPES, combine the flour, milk, water, eggs and butter in a mixing bowl. Add the chopped herbs and salt and mix until smooth. Chill, covered, for 30 minutes or longer.

Spray an omelet pan with nonstick cooking spray and preheat over medium-high heat. Pour about 2 tablespoons of the batter at a time into the pan and tilt the pan to spread evenly. Cook for 30 to 60 seconds or until the batter begins to bubble and the edges are cooked. Loosen the crêpe carefully from the pan with a spatula and turn. Cook for 30 to 60 seconds longer or until pale yellow and barely brown in spots. Remove from the pan and cool.

CRAWFISH SAUTÉ WITH POPCORN RICE CAKES

POPCORN RICE CAKES

2 tablespoons unsalted butter
1 teaspoon minced garlic
1 cup uncooked popcorn rice
1 1/2 cups water
salt to taste
1 medium onion, finely chopped
2 ribs celery, finely chopped
1 green bell pepper, finely chopped
8 ounces cooked crawfish tails,
    peeled, deveined
2 tablespoons unsalted butter
pepper to taste

CRAWFISH SAUTÉ

2 tablespoons unsalted butter
1 pound peeled cooked crawfish
    tails, deveined (about 4 pounds
    live crawfish)
1 red bell pepper, finely chopped
1 green bell pepper, finely chopped
1/2 cup chopped green onions
1 tablespoon Creole seafood
    seasoning
1 tablespoon Worcestershire sauce
1 cup (2 sticks) unsalted
    butter, softened

GARNISH

4 whole boiled crawfish

■ *Serves 4*

FOR THE POPCORN RICE CAKES, melt 2 tablespoons butter in a heavy saucepot over low heat. Add the garlic and sauté for 2 minutes. Add the rice and stir to coat well. Add the water and salt and bring to a boil. Simmer, tightly covered, for 20 minutes or until the rice is tender and the liquid is absorbed. Cool to room temperature.

Sauté the onion, celery, bell pepper and crawfish in 2 tablespoons butter in a large sauté pan until the vegetables are translucent. Stir in 1/3 of the cooked rice; reserve the remaining rice for another use. Season with pepper.

Process the mixture in a food processor until coarsely chopped. Shape into 4 large or 8 small cakes.

FOR THE CRAWFISH SAUTÉ, melt 2 tablespoons butter in a large sauté pan. Add the crawfish tails, bell peppers, green onions, Creole seasoning and Worcestershire sauce. Sauté just until the vegetables are tender; do not overcook.

Remove from the heat. Add 1 cup butter a small amount at a time, mixing until completely incorporated after each addition.

Serve immediately with the Popcorn Rice Cakes and garnish with a whole crawfish.

This Crawfish Sauté is a simple but spectacular dish—ideal for elegant entertaining. It's quick to assemble and all the ingredients can be prepared ahead of time. The final preparation takes only two minutes. Be sure not to overcook your crawfish. They're more delicate than shrimp and require more care in cooking.

PORK GRILLADES WITH ANDOUILLE GOAT CHEESE GRITS

ANDOUILLE GOAT CHEESE GRITS

4 cups water
3/4 cup white grits
1 cup ground or chopped
    precooked andouille, chorizo or
    spicy smoked sausage
1/4 cup heavy cream
1/3 cup butter
4 ounces goat cheese
1 tablespoon chopped fresh parsley
1/2 teaspoon kosher salt
1/4 teaspoon cracked black pepper

GRILLADE SAUCE

3 cups veal stock (page 199)
1/4 cup (1/2 stick) butter
6 tablespoons all-purpose flour
1 tablespoon vegetable oil
1/2 teaspoon minced garlic
1/4 cup finely chopped carrots
1/3 cup finely chopped onion
1/2 cup finely chopped celery
stems of 1 pint mushrooms
1/2 cup red wine
1 bay leaf
4 black peppercorns
4 sprigs of fresh thyme
stems of 1 bunch parsley
2 tablespoons Madeira

FOR THE GRITS, bring the water to a boil in a medium saucepot. Add the grits gradually, whisking constantly. Simmer for 30 minutes or until thickened, whisking occasionally.

Stir in the andouille and increase the heat to medium. Stir in the cream and butter. Fold in the goat cheese and parsley. Season with kosher salt and pepper.

FOR THE SAUCE, cook the veal stock in a saucepot until reduced by 1/2; set aside. Melt the butter in a small saucepot over medium heat and whisk in the flour gradually. Cook over low heat for 15 minutes to make a roux with a pale golden color and toasty smell, whisking constantly.

Heat the vegetable oil in a medium saucepot over medium-high heat. Add the garlic, carrots, onion, celery and mushroom stems. Cook until the onion is caramelized and the vegetables are tender. Add the red wine, stirring to deglaze the saucepot.

Add the bay leaf, peppercorns, thyme and parsley stems. Simmer until reduced by 1/2, stirring constantly. Add the reduced veal stock and bring to a boil, skimming the surface.

Stir a small amount of the grillade sauce into the roux, then stir the roux into the grillade sauce. Simmer for 10 minutes or until slightly thickened, stirring constantly. Stir in the Madeira. Remove from the heat and let stand for 10 minutes. Strain through a fine strainer.

PORK GRILLADES

2 pounds pork loin, sliced
    1 inch thick
1/2 cup all-purpose flour
2 tablespoons Creole seasoning
1/4 cup vegetable oil
1 tablespoon chopped garlic
1 cup julienned red onion
1 cup mixed julienned green, red
    and yellow bell peppers
1 cup sliced mixed mushrooms
1/4 cup brandy
2 tablespoons heavy whipping
    cream
1 tablespoon chopped fresh thyme
6 tablespoons (3/4 stick) butter,
    chilled, chopped
kosher salt and cracked black
    pepper to taste
2 tablespoons chopped green
    onions

■ *Serves 4*

FOR THE GRILLADES, pound the pork slices between 2 pieces of plastic wrap with a meat mallet. Coat with a mixture of the flour and Creole seasoning, shaking to remove any excess. Heat the vegetable oil in a large skillet or sauté pan. Add the pork and cook over medium heat until brown on both sides. Move to one side of the skillet.

Add the garlic, onion, bell peppers and mushrooms to the skillet and cook until the vegetables are tender. Add the brandy and ignite.

Allow the flames to subside and stir in the Grillade Sauce, heavy cream and thyme. Simmer for 5 to 10 minutes or until heated through. Add the butter a few pieces at a time, stirring constantly; the sauce will thicken. Season with kosher salt and pepper.

To serve, spoon several pieces of pork onto each plate. Top with a generous amount of the Grillade Sauce and sprinkle with the chopped green onions. Serve with the Andouille Goat Cheese Grits.

Although grillade is used in the singular in French, locals use the plural form. In Creole cooking, grillades were traditionally prepared with round steak, smothered with tomato and other vegetables and served with grits. Grillades and grits, cooked any style, are great for brunch, lunch or dinner. For a lighter version of the dish, use roasted corn, fresh thyme or green onions instead of the andouille and goat cheese to flavor the grits.

CHICKEN PONTALBA

BÉARNAISE SAUCE

2 cups (4 sticks) butter
1 cup chopped tarragon
1 tablespoon chopped shallots
1 cup red wine vinegar
1 teaspoon cracked black pepper
5 egg yolks
1/4 cup water
1/2 teaspoon salt
cracked black pepper to taste
salt to taste

CHICKEN

2 chickens
Creole seasoning to taste
1/4 cup (1/2 stick) butter, sliced into
    tablespoons

PONTALBA POTATOES

vegetable oil for frying
2 Idaho potatoes, peeled, chopped
    into 1/4-inch pieces
1 tablespoon blend of 80%
    vegetable oil and 20% olive oil
1 tablespoon chopped garlic
1 cup sliced mushrooms
1 cup chopped ham
Creole seasoning
1/2 cup sliced green onions

GARNISH

1 teaspoon chopped fresh parsley

■ *Serves 4*

FOR THE SAUCE, melt the butter in a sauté pan and skim off the cloudy foam. Scoop the clear butter off the milk solids which sink to the bottom of the pan. Cool slightly.

Combine the tarragon, shallots, wine vinegar and 1 teaspoon pepper in a saucepan and cook over medium heat until the vinegar evaporates. Cool to room temperature.

Whisk the egg yolks, water and 1/2 teaspoon salt in a double boiler or metal bowl placed over a saucepan of boiling water. Cook until the mixture is about three times the original volume and pale yellow, whisking constantly. Remove from the heat and whisk in the warm clarified butter gradually until the sauce is pale yellow, thick and creamy. Stir in the reduced vinegar mixture. Adjust the pepper and salt to taste. Cover and keep warm.

FOR THE CHICKEN, cut up the chickens, removing the breasts and the legs with the thigh portion. Debone the chickens. Season with Creole seasoning. Place the thigh and leg portions on a work surface and place 1 chicken breast on each thigh portion. Wrap the thigh portion around the breast portion to form a ball and arrange on a lightly greased baking sheet. Sprinkle with Creole seasoning and place 1 tablespoon of butter on each. Roast at 350 degrees for 25 minutes or until cooked through.

FOR THE PONTALBA POTATOES, preheat the vegetable oil to 350 degrees in a deep fryer. Add the potatoes and deep-fry until golden brown; drain. Heat 1 tablespoon oil blend in a medium sauté pan and add the garlic. Sauté until golden brown. Add the mushrooms and ham and sauté until the mushrooms are tender. Add the fried potatoes and sauté until heated through. Season with Creole seasoning and stir in the green onions. Cook for 1 to 2 minutes.

To serve, spoon the Pontalba Potatoes onto the serving plates and place the chicken on the potatoes. Top with warm Béarnaise Sauce and sprinkle with the parsley.

FRESH FRUIT BEIGNETS

RUM CRÈME ANGLAISE

1 cup milk
1 cup cream
1/2 cup sugar
6 egg yolks
3 tablespoons dark rum

BEIGNETS

1/4 cup (1/2 stick) butter
3 cups fresh fruit
sugar to taste
2 sheets frozen puff pastry, thawed
vegetable oil for frying

■ *Makes 12*

FOR THE RUM CRÈME ANGLAISE, combine the milk, cream and sugar in a medium saucepan and bring to a simmer. Beat the egg yolks in a medium stainless steel mixing bowl and place the bowl over a saucepan of simmering water. Whisk the hot milk mixture very gradually into the egg yolks. Cook over medium heat until the sauce thickens to the consistency of custard, stirring constantly with a wooden spoon. Remove from the heat and stir in the rum. Chill, covered, until serving time.

FOR THE BEIGNETS, melt the butter in a large sauté pan and add the fruit. Cook until the natural juices are rendered and reduced to a thick syrup. Stir in sugar and remove from the heat.

Cut each sheet of puff pastry into 6 squares to form 12 squares. Spoon about 1/4 cup of the fruit into the center of each square. Fold up the corners of each square to form a pouch to enclose the fruit; seal by pinching gently along the seams. Brush with a small amount of water if necessary and rub gently with your fingertips.

Heat the vegetable oil to 350 degrees in a deep fryer. Add the beignets in batches and deep-fry for 10 minutes or until golden brown; remove with a slotted spoon to paper towels to drain.

To serve, spoon the rum crème anglaise onto the serving plates and place the hot beignets in the center of the plates.

Use strawberries, blueberries, peaches, apples or whatever is in season and whatever you like best for these Fresh Fruit Beignets. The amount of sugar needed depends on the fruit and individual tastes. This also makes a great dessert when served hot with a scoop of ice cream.

LOST BREAD

APPLE PECAN SAUCE WITH ANDOUILLE SAUSAGE

1 1/4 cups pecan pieces
1 cup (2 sticks) butter
1/2 (1-pound) package dark
    brown sugar
1/2 cup honey
2 tablespoons butter
8 ounces andouille sausage, sliced
2 Granny Smith apples, cored,
    sliced

LOST BREAD

4 eggs
2 cups milk
2 tablespoons sugar
1/8 teaspoon cinnamon
1/8 teaspoon nutmeg
pinch of salt
8 (3/4-inch) slices day-old French
    bread
1 tablespoon butter, sliced into
    4 pats

GARNISH

confectioners' sugar

■ *Serves 4*

FOR THE SAUCE, spread the pecans evenly on a small baking sheet and toast lightly in a 300-degree oven to release the oils and crisp. Combine 1 cup butter, brown sugar and honey in a small saucepot and bring to a boil. Remove from the heat and mix well. Stir in the pecans.

Melt 2 tablespoons butter in a skillet over high heat. Add the sausage and cook until brown on both sides. Add the apples and cook for 1 to 2 minutes or until tender. Stir in the pecan mixture and cook until heated through; keep warm.

FOR THE BREAD, whisk the eggs in a small bowl. Add the milk, sugar, cinnamon, nutmeg and salt and mix well. Place the bread slices in the egg mixture and allow to stand for about 1 minute, coating both sides evenly.

Preheat a nonstick skillet over medium heat. Melt a small pat of butter in the skillet and add 2 slices of the bread. Fry until golden brown on both sides and cooked through. Remove to an ovenproof serving plate and keep warm in a 200-degree oven. Repeat with the remaining bread, adding a pat of butter to the skillet between batches.

To serve, place 2 slices of bread on each serving plate. Spoon the Apple Pecan Sauce with Andouille Sausage over the bread. Garnish with a sprinkle of confectioners' sugar.

You can find this great breakfast and brunch dish on both the children's and regular menus at the restaurant. It gets its name, Pain Perdu in French, from its use of day-old—or lost—French bread.

45

BRIOCHE

INGREDIENTS

7 eggs
3 tablespoons sugar
3 tablespoons fast-rising instant
    dry yeast
4 cups (or more) high-gluten
    bread flour
2 teaspoons salt
1 cup (2 sticks) butter, softened
1 egg, lightly beaten

■ *Makes 24 rolls or 2 loaves*

Beat 7 eggs lightly with the sugar and yeast in a mixing bowl. Combine with the bread flour and salt in the bowl of a mixer fitted with a dough hook or paddle attachment. Mix at low speed to form a stiff dough. Add the softened butter a few tablespoons at a time, mixing constantly. Beat at medium speed for 10 minutes longer or until the surface of the dough is smooth and little of the mixture adheres to the bottom of the bowl, adding 1 to 2 tablespoons additional flour if necessary.

Remove to a greased bowl, turning to coat the surface, and cover loosely with plastic wrap. Let rise in a warm place for 30 minutes or until doubled in bulk.

To bake rolls, punch down the dough and shape into 24 balls. Place in greased muffin cups and brush the tops with lightly beaten egg. Cover loosely with plastic wrap and let rise until doubled in bulk. Bake at 350 degrees for 25 minutes or until golden brown.

To bake loaves, punch down the dough and shape into 2 loaves. Place in 4×9-inch loaf pans; the dough should not reach higher than halfway up the sides. Cover loosely with plastic wrap and let rise until doubled in bulk. Bake at 350 degrees for 35 to 40 minutes or until golden brown.

SKILLET CORNBREAD

INGREDIENTS

1 cup cornmeal
1 cup all-purpose flour
3 tablespoons baking powder
1 teaspoon salt
3 eggs, lightly beaten
1/4 cup (1/2 stick) butter, melted,
    cooled
11/2 cups buttermilk
1/3 cup sour cream
1/4 cup each finely chopped red
    and green bell pepper
1/2 cup fresh corn kernels

■ *Serves 8*

Mix the cornmeal, flour, baking powder and salt in a medium bowl. Add the eggs, melted butter, buttermilk and sour cream and mix just until smooth. Stir in the bell peppers and corn.

Preheat the oven to 375 degrees. Pour the batter into a greased 9-inch cast-iron skillet or 8×8-inch baking dish. Bake for 25 to 30 minutes or until golden brown.

You may glaze Skillet Cornbread with a mixture of 2 tablespoons melted butter and 2 tablespoons honey brushed over the top.

POTATO ROLLS

INGREDIENTS

2 tablespoons sugar
1 tablespoon instant dry yeast
1/4 cup water
1/2 cup milk
1/4 cup (1/2 stick) butter, softened
1 egg
11/4 cups mashed cooked potatoes
3 cups all-purpose flour
1 teaspoon salt

■ *Makes 24 rolls*

Sprinkle the sugar and yeast over the water in a mixing bowl fitted with a dough hook and let stand until mixture bubbles. Add the milk, butter, egg, potatoes, flour and salt. Mix at medium speed to form a slightly sticky dough.

Place dough on a work surface lightly dusted with additional flour and sprinkle the top liberally with flour. Knead briefly; the dough should be soft and sticky. Place in a greased bowl, turning to coat the surface. Cover loosely with plastic wrap and let rise in a warm place for 20 to 30 minutes or until doubled in bulk.

Punch down the dough on a floured surface and shape into 24 balls. Place in greased muffin cups. Cover loosely with plastic wrap and let rise in a warm place for 20 to 30 minutes or until doubled in bulk. Bake at 350 degrees for 25 to 30 minutes or until golden brown.

Potato Rolls are perfect for making miniature muffulettas that are great to serve at parties. A muffuletta is a New Orleans-style sandwich filled with Italian meats, cheeses and olive salad.

ONION BREAD

INGREDIENTS

3 medium onions
2 tablespoons butter
1 tablespoon sugar
1 package instant dry yeast
2 cups water
8 cups (or more) all-purpose flour
1 tablespoon salt

■ *Makes 2 loaves*

Slice the onions into 1/4-inch slivers. Cook in the butter in a sauté pan until caramelized and golden brown. Cool to room temperature.

Combine the sugar, yeast and water in a medium mixing bowl and let stand until the mixture bubbles. Add the flour and salt; mix with a dough hook attachment or knead by hand to form a stiff dough. Add the onions and mix until smooth, adding additional flour 1 tablespoon at a time if necessary to form a dough that cleans the bottom of the bowl.

Place in a greased bowl, turning to coat the surface. Cover loosely with plastic wrap and let rise for 45 to 60 minutes or until doubled in bulk. Punch down the dough on a floured surface and shape into 2 loaves.

Place the loaves on a baking sheet and make several 1/4-inch-deep cuts across the top of each with a sharp knife. Cover loosely with plastic wrap and let rise for 45 to 60 minutes or until doubled in bulk. Bake at 350 degrees for 40 minutes or until the loaves are golden brown and sound hollow when the bottoms are tapped.

PONCHATOULA STRAWBERRY PECAN MUFFINS

INGREDIENTS

4 cups all-purpose flour
2 tablespoons baking powder
1/8 teaspoon salt
1/2 cup (1 stick) butter, softened
1 cup sugar
2 eggs
1 cup milk
2 cups sliced fresh strawberries
1 cup chopped pecans

■ *Makes 2 dozen*

Preheat the oven to 350 degrees. Whisk the flour, baking powder and salt in a medium bowl. Cream the butter and sugar with an electric mixer in a large mixing bowl until light and fluffy. Beat in the eggs one at a time.

Add the dry ingredients alternately with the milk, beating just until mixed after each addition. The batter will be slightly sticky; do not overmix. Fold in the strawberries and pecans. Spoon into greased muffin cups, filling 3/4 full. Bake for 15 to 20 minutes or until golden brown.

This is our basic muffin mix. You may substitute other seasonal fruit such as blueberries, blackberries or peaches for the strawberries.

THE KITCHEN STAFF SPENDS THE HOURS BEFORE WE OPEN THE

DOORS PEELING AND SLICING VEGETABLES THAT ARRIVED THAT

MORNING AND PREPARING THE FRESH TUNA AND OTHER FRESH CATCH.

GULF OYSTERS ARE SELECTED AND READIED. EVERYONE MOVES IN

PRECISE SYNCHRONIZATION, PAYING ATTENTION TO THE SMALLEST

DETAIL IN PREPARING EACH DISH. ONE LAST CHECK AND WE'RE READY.

APPETIZERS

THE COOKING SCHOOL AT
BLACKBERRY FARM

Walland, Tennessee

Blackberry Farm, one of the country's finest country inn resorts, nestled in the

Great Smoky Mountains, has been ranked as one of the top four inns in

America by *Zagat* and one of the top four North American small hotels by *Condé Nast*

Traveler. It draws an elite clientele with one of its chief attractions being

cooking classes taught by guest chefs. The classes culminate in a

lunch featuring the recipes taught during the course. In the summer of 2001,

Executive Chef Gus Martin packed up nearly 150 pounds

of fresh redfish, lump crabmeat, gulf shrimp, oysters and other local

Louisiana products, and flew to Tennessee to share recipes for some of

Palace Café's signature dishes with a group of 25 food lovers.

MENU

Crabmeat Cheesecake with Pecan Crust

Seafood Court-Bouillon

Banana Beignets with Foster Sauce

FOURTH OF JULY GALA DINNER, UNITED STATES EMBASSY

Ottawa, Canada

In 1998, the United States Embassy in Canada asked the state of Louisiana

to host its Fourth of July Celebration Gala. Lieutenant Governor Kathleen Blanco invited

Palace Café and Executive Chef Martin and Haley Gabel of Ralph Brennan's Bacco to

provide the food for the occasion. Dignitaries from throughout Canada, American citizens

in the area and many others feasted on cuisine we like to call the *Flavor of New Orleans*.

MENU

Masa Fried Oysters with Horseradish Cream
Crawfish Bruschetta
Andouille with Caramelized Onions and Creole Mustard Dipping Sauce
Fried Crab Cakes

Crawfish Risotto

Muscovy Duck Cannelloni

Baby Greens and Chicory Farms Goat Cheese Salad

Garlic-Crusted Gulf Fish

Praline Ice Cream Sandwich

RED BEAN DIP

INGREDIENTS

1 pound dried red beans
2 tablespoons butter
8 ounces andouille sausage,
    chopped
1 cup chopped celery
1 1/2 cups chopped onions
1 cup chopped green bell pepper
1/4 cup chopped garlic
1 teaspoon chopped fresh thyme
2 bay leaves
2 tablespoons Creole seasoning
8 cups water

■ *Serves 8 to 12*

Sort and rinse the dried beans. Combine the beans with enough water to cover in a large bowl and let stand for 8 hours or longer.

Melt the butter in a large saucepan and add the andouille. Cook until the sausage is light brown. Add the celery, onions, bell pepper, garlic, thyme, bay leaves and Creole seasoning. Sauté until the vegetables are tender.

Drain the beans and add to the saucepan with 8 cups water. Cook over medium-high heat for 1 hour or until the beans are tender, stirring occasionally.

Purée the mixture in batches in a food processor and return to the saucepan. Reduce the heat and simmer for 5 to 6 hours or until thick enough to dip with chips. Serve warm with potato chips.

We've even found a way to "Creolize" bean dip by adding our own Creole seasoning blend (page 201) and some andouille sausage to give it a little more spice. This dish was on our first menu at Palace Café and still makes frequent appearances. It's a must for game day or other casual gatherings, and is a favorite for the kids. You may substitute smoked sausage, smoked ham or pickled pork for the andouille sausage in the recipe if you like. Remember, if you use pickled pork, rinse or blanch it first. Otherwise, it will make the dip too salty.

ALLIGATOR POTPIE

POTPIE CRUST

2 1/2 cups all-purpose flour
2 1/2 cups cake flour
1/4 cup sugar
1 teaspoon salt
1 egg yolk
1 cup (2 sticks) butter, chilled
1/2 cup shortening
3/4 cup ice water

POTPIE FILLING

1 cup all-purpose flour
1/3 cup Creole seasoning
1 pound alligator tail meat, chopped
1/2 cup (about) vegetable oil
1 tablespoon chopped garlic
4 bay leaves
1/2 teaspoon crushed red pepper
2 cups finely chopped onions
1 cup mixed finely chopped green,
    red and yellow bell peppers
1/2 cup Madeira
3 cups chicken stock (page 197) or
    canned chicken broth
1 tablespoon chopped fresh thyme
1 cup sliced green onions
kosher salt and cracked black
    pepper to taste
1 egg, beaten

■ *Serves 8*

FOR THE CRUST, mix the all-purpose flour, cake flour, sugar, salt and egg yolk in a large stainless steel bowl. Cut in the chilled butter and shortening with a pastry cutter or 2 knives until the mixture is in pieces the size of small peas. Pour the ice water over the mixture and squeeze with your hands to form a dough with small bits of butter still visible; do not overmix. Wrap in plastic wrap and chill for 2 hours or longer.

FOR THE FILLING, whisk the flour and Creole seasoning in a bowl. Add the alligator meat and mix to coat well, shaking off any excess.

Heat just enough vegetable oil to cover the bottom of a large sauté pan. Add the alligator meat and sauté until golden brown. Add the garlic, bay leaves, red pepper, onions and bell peppers. Sauté until the vegetables are tender.

Add the wine to the sauté pan, stirring to deglaze. Stir in the chicken stock and bring to a simmer. Simmer until thickened. Stir in the thyme and green onions. Season with kosher salt and cracked pepper and cool to room temperature; discard the bay leaves.

To assemble and cook, grease 8 ramekins or other ovenproof baking dishes. Place the pie dough on a floured surface and roll enough to cut 8 circles to cover the bottoms and sides of the ramekins, reserving the remaining dough. Fit the circles into the ramekins and trim the edges.

Spoon the filling into the prepared ramekins. Roll the reserved dough 1/4 inch thick and cut with a sharp floured knife into strips to fit the tops of the ramekins. Arrange the strips in a lattice design over the pies; trim or tuck the edges. Brush the tops with the egg and bake at 350 degrees for 20 minutes or until the crust is golden brown.

This is the Creole version of chicken potpie. However, let there be no mistake, alligator does NOT taste like chicken; it tastes like alligator. Alligator season in Louisiana is September and October.

BLACKENED CATFISH WITH
SWEET POTATO HASH

SWEET POTATO HASH

2 large sweet potatoes, cooked
1 tablespoon butter
1/2 tablespoon finely chopped garlic
1 cup finely chopped tasso
1 cup thinly sliced leeks
1 cup mixed finely chopped green,
    red and yellow bell peppers
1 tablespoon cane vinegar or apple
    cider vinegar
1/2 cup thinly sliced green onions
1 tablespoon chopped fresh oregano
2 tablespoons molasses
salt and pepper to taste

CATFISH

18 (2- to 3-ounce) catfish fillets, or
    larger fillets cut into strips
1/4 cup Creole seasoning
1/4 cup vegetable oil
Crystal Beurre Blanc (page 61)

■ *Serves 6*

FOR THE HASH, chop the cooled sweet potatoes. Melt the butter in a large sauté pan and add the garlic. Sauté until golden brown. Add the tasso and cook until brown.

Stir in the leeks and bell peppers. Cook until the vegetables begin to get tender. Add the sweet potatoes and cane vinegar. Cook over medium heat for 5 to 7 minutes. Stir in the green onions, oregano and molasses. Season with salt and pepper. Keep warm.

FOR THE CATFISH, preheat a cast-iron skillet over high heat. Sprinkle the catfish fillets generously with the Creole seasoning and rub the seasoning in to coat both sides evenly. Add the vegetable oil to the hot skillet. Add the fillets and cook for 2 minutes on each side or until blackened.

Spoon the hash onto the serving plates and arrange 3 fillets on each serving. Drizzle with Crystal Beurre Blanc.

At Palace Café, we love to cook with fresh catfish from Des Allemandes, Louisiana. This dish makes a great appetizer, or an entrée if you use larger catfish fillets. Be sure that the vent on the stove is on while you are blackening food, or even open a window. Don't be surprised if the fish creates a good bit of smoke: it's supposed to! Our chef, Gus Martin, prepared this dish at Jazz Fest 2000 and set off the smoke detectors in the grandstand at the Fairgrounds. The fact that he was invited back to cook the following year should tell you how great this dish is!

Cast-iron skillets work best for blackening food. Aluminum skillets can also be used, but a pan with a nonstick coating will not blacken food properly. It's important to season the food generously and evenly with Creole seasoning and to maintain a high temperature.

FRIED CRAB CAKES

INGREDIENTS

1 cup (2 sticks) butter
1 tablespoon chopped garlic
1/2 cup mixed finely chopped green, red and yellow bell peppers
1/2 cup finely chopped onion
1/2 cup finely chopped celery
2 bay leaves
1 teaspoon fresh thyme
1 pound crab claw meat
1 tablespoon Creole seasoning
2 teaspoons cracked black pepper
3 cups bread crumbs processed from stale French bread or white bread
1/2 cup chopped green onions
kosher salt to taste
2 cups all-purpose flour
1 tablespoon Creole seasoning
2 cups bread crumbs processed from stale French bread or white bread
1 tablespoon Creole seasoning
4 eggs
2 cups milk
vegetable oil for frying or sautéing

■ *Serves 8*

Melt the butter in a large saucepan over medium heat and add the garlic, bell peppers, onion, celery, bay leaves and thyme. Sauté for about 10 minutes or until the vegetables are tender. Stir in the crabmeat, 1 tablespoon Creole seasoning and cracked pepper. Cook just until the crabmeat is heated through. Stir in 3 cups bread crumbs and green onions. Remove from the heat and season with kosher salt; discard the bay leaves. Cool to room temperature.

Season the flour with 1 tablespoon Creole seasoning in a bowl. Season 2 cups bread crumbs with 1 tablespoon Creole seasoning in a bowl. Whisk the eggs and milk in a bowl. Shape the crabmeat mixture into tightly compressed 3-ounce cakes. Coat the cakes with the flour mixture, dip them into the egg wash, then press both sides into the bread crumb mixture.

Heat the vegetable oil in a deep fryer or skillet and add the crab cakes. Deep-fry or sauté until golden brown on both sides.

We like using the sweeter claw meat rather than jumbo lump crabmeat for these cakes. Serve them as a casual appetizer with Creole Tomato Tartar Sauce (page 76) or Ravigote Sauce (page 61), or on a bed of greens for a great entrée salad with Fresh Herb Vinaigrette (page 108). They're also good served in big bowls of Blue Crab Soft-Shell Bisque (page 95), garnished with jumbo lump crabmeat or crab fingers for an elegant entrée soup.

CRABMEAT CHEESECAKE WITH PECAN CRUST

PECAN CRUST

3/4 cup pecans
1 cup all-purpose flour
1/4 teaspoon salt
5 tablespoons butter, chilled
3 tablespoons ice water

FILLING

1/2 cup finely chopped onion
1 tablespoon butter
4 ounces crabmeat
8 ounces cream cheese, softened
1/3 cup Creole Cream Cheese
    (page 176) or sour cream
2 eggs
1 tablespoon Crystal hot sauce
kosher salt and white pepper to taste

MEUNIÈRE SAUCE WITH MUSHROOMS

1 lemon, peeled, cut into quarters
1/2 cup Worcestershire sauce
1/2 cup Crystal hot sauce
1/4 cup heavy whipping cream
1 pound (4 sticks) butter, chopped
kosher salt and white pepper to taste
2 cups sliced mixed wild mushrooms
2 tablespoons butter

GARNISH

sautéed crab claw fingers

■ *Serves 8*

FOR THE CRUST, preheat the oven to 350 degrees. Grind the pecans fine in a food processor. Add the flour and salt and process to mix. Remove to a large mixing bowl and cut in the butter with 2 knives until the mixture resembles small peas. Add the ice water and mix just until the dough holds together.

Roll the dough 1/8 inch thick on a lightly floured surface. Press into a lightly greased 9-inch tart pan, starting with the side and then the bottom. Bake for 20 minutes or until golden brown.

FOR THE FILLING, reduce the oven temperature to 300 degrees. Sauté the onion in the butter in a sauté pan until translucent. Add the crabmeat and cook just until heated through; remove from the heat.

Beat the cream cheese in a mixer fitted with a paddle or with a wooden spoon until smooth. Add the Creole Cream Cheese and mix well. Mix in the eggs one at a time. Fold in the crabmeat mixture gently. Stir in the pepper sauce and season with kosher salt and white pepper.

Spoon the filling into the prepared crust and bake for 30 to 40 minutes or until firm to the touch.

FOR THE SAUCE, combine the lemon, Worcestershire sauce and pepper sauce in a heavy saucepot. Cook over medium heat until thick and syrupy, stirring constantly with a wire whisk. Whisk in the cream.

Reduce the heat to low and add 1 pound butter one piece at a time, mixing until completely incorporated before adding more butter. Remove from the heat and stir until very smooth. Season with kosher salt and white pepper. Strain through a fine strainer and keep warm.

Sauté the mushrooms in 2 tablespoons butter in a skillet until the mushrooms are tender and the moisture has completely evaporated; excess moisture from the mushrooms may cause the sauce to break when the mushrooms are added. Stir the mushrooms into the sauce.

To serve, slice the cheesecake and place on serving plates. Top each serving with the warm sauce and garnish with 3 sautéed crab claw fingers.

*C*rabmeat Cheesecake with Pecan Crust is one of our signature dishes at Palace Café and one of our most requested recipes. It's served here with Oyster Shooters (page 69). It's also great as an hors d'oeuvre when cut and served in bite-size pieces. We like to garnish it with crab claw fingers lightly sautéed in butter.

If the dough for the Pecan Crust is made in advance, wrap it in plastic wrap and store it in the refrigerator. Allow it to return to room temperature before rolling it.

59

SEARED CRAB CAKES WITH CORN RELISH

CORN RELISH

1 or 2 ears fresh corn
1 tablespoon butter
1/2 cup finely chopped red onion
1/2 cup mixed finely chopped green,
    red and yellow bell peppers
1 cup thinly sliced green onions
1 teaspoon chopped fresh thyme
2 tablespoons vegetable oil
2 tablespoons cane vinegar
salt and cracked black pepper
    to taste

FOR THE CORN RELISH, cut enough kernels from the corncobs with a sharp knife to measure 1 cup. Sauté the corn in the butter in a large sauté pan just until the kernels start to brown. Cool to room temperature.

Combine the corn with the onion, bell peppers, green onions, thyme, vegetable oil, cane vinegar, salt and cracked pepper in a bowl and mix well.

RAVIGOTE SAUCE

1 tablespoon chopped capers
1 tablespoon horseradish
1/2 cup mayonnaise
1 tablespoon Creole mustard
1/4 teaspoon Crystal hot sauce
1/4 teaspoon Worcestershire sauce
juice of 1/4 lemon
1 tablespoon finely chopped
    red onion
salt and pepper to taste

FOR THE SAUCE, combine the capers, horseradish, mayonnaise, Creole mustard, hot sauce, Worcestershire sauce and lemon juice in a bowl and blend until smooth. Stir in the onion and season to taste.

CRYSTAL BEURRE BLANC

1 cup Crystal hot sauce
1/4 cup heavy cream
2 cups (4 sticks) butter, chilled,
    chopped

FOR THE BEURRE BLANC, cook the hot sauce in a saucepot over medium-high heat until reduced to a syrupy consistency, whisking constantly to avoid burning. Whisk in the cream and reduce the heat to low. Add the butter a few pieces at a time, whisking constantly to incorporate completely after each addition. Cook until completely smooth, whisking constantly to keep the mixture from breaking.

CRAB CAKES

8 ounces mixed wild mushrooms,
    such as button, shiitake, oyster,
    crimimi and portobello, sliced
    into bite-size pieces
1 teaspoon kosher salt
1 teaspoon freshly cracked
    black pepper
1/4 cup vegetable oil
1 pound jumbo lump crabmeat
1 cup sliced green onions
1/2 cup Ravigote Sauce
1/4 cup vegetable oil

CRAB FINGERS

1 tablespoon butter
8 ounces crab fingers

GARNISH

8 sprigs of fresh thyme

■ *Serves 8*

FOR THE CRAB CAKES, preheat the oven to 350 degrees. Toss the mushrooms with the salt, pepper and 1/4 cup vegetable oil in a bowl. Spread on a baking sheet and roast for 10 to 15 minutes or until they begin to dry. Cool to room temperature.

Combine the roasted mushrooms with the crabmeat, green onions and 1/2 cup Ravigote Sauce in a small mixing bowl. Chill for 30 minutes.

Heat 1/4 cup vegetable oil in a cast-iron skillet over medium-high heat. Fill eight 3-ounce stainless steel rings with the crabmeat mixture and place the rings in the heated oil, using a spatula to keep the crabmeat from falling from the bottoms of the rings.

Sear the crab cakes for about 2 minutes. Slide the spatula beneath each crab cake and cover the top with a second spatula to turn the cakes, gently sliding them at an angle off the spatula and into the skillet to avoid splashing the oil. Sear for 2 minutes longer. Place the skillet in the oven and bake for 5 to 10 minutes or until the crab cakes are cooked through. Keep warm.

FOR THE CRAB FINGERS, heat the butter in a small sauté pan and add the crab fingers. Sauté just until heated through.

To serve, ladle Crystal Beurre Blanc onto the centers of 8 serving plates, spreading evenly with the ladle. Place 1 crab cake in the sauce and gently remove the ring. Top with the corn relish and crab fingers. Garnish with thyme.

Our chefs have evolved the recipe for Crab Cakes over the years, and it just keeps getting better and better. These Seared Crab Cakes are a lighter, dressier version of the more traditional breaded and fried crab cakes. Without the breading, the flavor of the crabmeat can really be tasted. This is a great recipe to experiment with— if you don't like mushrooms, leave them out and increase the amount of crabmeat used. Just let the cakes cook a little bit longer. For a slightly sweeter Corn Relish, grill the corn in the husks instead of sautéing it.

CRAB AND CRAWFISH CHOPS
WITH CREOLE RAGOÛT

CREOLE RAGOÛT

2 or 3 large Creole tomatoes
2 tablespoons vegetable oil
1 tablespoon butter
1 teaspoon chopped garlic
1/2 cup finely chopped onion
1/2 cup mixed chopped green, red
    and yellow bell peppers
1/2 cup fresh corn kernels
1 cup sliced okra
1 teaspoon Creole seasoning
3/4 cup crab stock (page 196)
1 tablespoon chopped fresh thyme
1/2 cup (1 stick) butter, chilled
kosher salt and cracked black
    pepper to taste

CRAB AND CRAWFISH CHOPS

8 ounces crawfish tails, chopped
8 ounces jumbo lump crabmeat
8 ounces crab claw meat
1/4 cup equal parts chopped fresh
    basil, thyme and oregano
1/2 cup mixed finely chopped green,
    red and yellow bell peppers
1 cup chopped green onions
1 cup mayonnaise
3 tablespoons Creole mustard
1/2 cup seasoned bread crumbs
11/2 tablespoons Creole seasoning
1 pound crab fingers
2 cups all-purpose flour
1 tablespoon Creole seasoning
4 eggs
2 cups milk
4 cups seasoned bread crumbs
vegetable oil for frying

GARNISH

4 bunches watercress

■ *Serves 8*

FOR THE RAGOÛT, core the tomatoes and cut into halves. Rub the skins with the vegetable oil and make a small slit in the skin of each. Place cut side down on a baking sheet. Roast at 400 degrees for 15 minutes or until the skins blister. Cool to room temperature, remove the skins and seeds and chop. Melt 1 tablespoon butter in a saucepot over medium heat. Add the garlic, onion, bell peppers, corn, okra and Creole seasoning. Cook for 15 to 20 minutes or until the vegetables are tender.

Add the roasted tomatoes and cook for 5 to 10 minutes longer. Stir in the crab stock and bring to a boil. Cook until the mixture begins to reduce; reduce the heat to medium-low and skim the surface. Stir in the thyme. Chop 1/2 cup butter and add several pieces at a time, whisking until completely incorporated after each addition. Cook until thickened and season with kosher salt and cracked pepper.

FOR THE CHOPS, combine the crawfish tails, lump crabmeat, crab claw meat, fresh herbs, bell peppers, green onions, mayonnaise, Creole mustard, 1/2 cup bread crumbs and 11/2 tablespoons Creole seasoning in a large mixing bowl and mix well. Add additional crumbs if necessary to bind. Chill for 30 minutes or longer.

Shape about 2 tablespoons of the crabmeat mixture around each crab finger to resemble a lamb or veal chop, leaving the shell "finger" of the crab finger uncovered to resemble the bone. Chill the chops for 15 to 30 minutes to set. Mix the flour with 1 tablespoon Creole seasoning. Blend the eggs with the milk in a bowl. Place 4 cups seasoned bread crumbs in a bowl. Coat the chops with the flour, shaking off any excess. Dip the chops into the egg wash and press into the bread crumbs, coating well; wipe off the breading from the shell "fingers."

Heat the vegetable oil in a skillet and add the chops. Fry until golden brown on both sides. Serve the chops with the Creole Ragoût and garnish with the watercress.

This Creole Ragoût also goes great with grilled or sautéed fish, crab cakes, fried oysters or soft-shell crab.

CRAWFISH WITH FRIED GREEN TOMATOES

CRAWFISH

1 cup heavy whipping cream
1 teaspoon chopped garlic
2 ounces finely chopped tasso
1 teaspoon butter
1/4 cup mixed finely chopped green,
    red and yellow bell peppers
1/4 cup half-moon leek slices
1 teaspoon Creole seasoning
8 ounces crawfish tails
2 tablespoons brandy
1 teaspoon chopped fresh thyme
1/2 cup chopped green onions
1 tablespoon butter, chilled

FRIED GREEN TOMATOES

1 cup all-purpose flour
1 to 2 teaspoons Creole seasoning
1 egg
1 cup milk
1 cup seasoned bread crumbs
2 large green tomatoes
vegetable oil for frying

GARNISH

4 sprigs of fresh thyme
4 boiled crawfish (optional)

■ *Serves 4*

FOR THE CRAWFISH, cook the cream in a small saucepot over medium heat until reduced by 1/2. Sauté the garlic and tasso in 1 teaspoon butter in a large saucepan over medium heat until the tasso begins to brown. Add the bell peppers, leeks and Creole seasoning. Sauté until the vegetables are tender-crisp.

Add the crawfish tails and brandy. Ignite the brandy and allow the flames to subside. Stir in the reduced cream, thyme and green onions. Reduce the heat and add the chilled butter, whisking constantly until thickened. Keep warm over low heat.

FOR THE TOMATOES, mix the flour with the Creole seasoning in a bowl. Whisk the egg and milk in a bowl. Pour the bread crumbs into a bowl. Cut each tomato into 1/2 inch thick slices, discarding the end pieces. Coat the slices with the seasoned flour. Dip in the egg wash and press into the bread crumbs to coat evenly.

Heat the vegetable oil in a skillet and add the tomato slices. Fry until golden brown on both sides. Drain on paper towels.

To serve, place a slice of green tomato in the center of each of 4 serving plates. Spoon the crawfish sauce over the slices and top with the remaining slices. Garnish with a sprig of fresh thyme and a boiled crawfish.

rawfish with Fried Green Tomatoes is a great quick and easy summertime dish. The green tomatoes have a tart sweetness that tastes even better with all the other flavors in the creamy crawfish sauce—the spicy, smoky tasso, the hint of brandy, the fresh thyme. If crawfish aren't in season or are not available, leave out the crawfish and increase the amount of tasso in the sauce. For a great vegetarian version, substitute wild mushrooms, such as crimini, shiitake, oyster or portobello, for the crawfish and the tasso. If you use portobellos, remember to scrape the black gills from the bottom of the caps to avoid turning the sauce black.

OYSTERS BIENVILLE

BIENVILLE SAUCE

4 slices bacon
3 tablespoons butter
1/2 cup finely chopped green onions
3/4 cup all-purpose flour
1 3/4 cups fish stock (page 199)
6 tablespoons white wine
1/2 teaspoon kosher salt
1/8 teaspoon cayenne pepper
2 egg yolks
1 cup finely chopped cooked shrimp
1 cup finely chopped mushrooms
2 teaspoons Worcestershire sauce
2 teaspoons finely chopped
    fresh parsley

OYSTERS

4 cups rock salt
24 freshly shucked oysters on the
    half-shell
white truffle oil (optional)

GARNISH

4 lemons, cut into 8 decorative
    crowns
8 sprigs of flat-leaf parsley

■ *Serves 8*

FOR THE SAUCE, fry the bacon in a skillet until crisp; drain the skillet, reserving 3 tablespoons of the drippings. Chop the bacon. Combine the reserved drippings and butter in a large saucepan and heat until the butter melts. Add the green onions and sauté for 5 to 10 minutes or until tender.

Stir in the bacon and flour and reduce the heat to low. Cook for 5 to 7 minutes or until bubbly but not brown, whisking constantly; remove from the heat. Whisk in the fish stock, wine, kosher salt and cayenne pepper.

Whisk in the egg yolks one at a time. Place over medium-high heat and add the shrimp, mushrooms, Worcestershire sauce and parsley. Reduce the heat to low and cook for 10 to 15 minutes or until of the desired consistency. Keep warm.

FOR THE OYSTERS, preheat the oven to 350 degrees. Place the rock salt in the bottoms of 8 small French pans or other baking dishes. Preheat the pans in the oven for 8 to 10 minutes to ensure the oysters cook through to their centers. Place 3 oysters in half-shells on the salt in each pan. Spoon or pipe the sauce over the oysters. Bake for 10 to 12 minutes or until golden brown. Drizzle with white truffle oil and garnish with lemon crowns and flat-leaf parsley.

Oysters Bienville is another old New Orleans classic that we've taken to another level. We add bacon to it to bring out the earthiness of the mushrooms. Then we finish the oysters with a drizzle of truffle oil for enhanced flavor and an unmistakable heavenly aroma that hits you as soon as the plate touches the table. On special occasions, we top the oysters with chopped truffles, which are expensive, but we think well worth it. We spoon the Bienville Sauce into a pastry bag and pipe it over the oysters, but it's just as good spooned over the top.

MASA FRIED OYSTERS

INGREDIENTS

3 cups flour
1 cup masa harina
1/4 cup Creole seasoning
1/2 cup cornstarch
2 pints oysters
vegetable oil for frying
sauces (below and page 67)

■ *Serves 6*

Mix the flour, masa harina, Creole seasoning and cornstarch in a large bowl. Coat the oysters with the flour mixture, shaking off any excess.

Heat the oil to 350 degrees. Fry one oyster to check the temperature of the oil; it should be golden brown, crisp and hot through to the center. Adjust the oil temperature; oysters will burn easily if the oil is too hot and will be greasy if the oil is not hot enough.

Fry the oysters in batches and drain on paper towels. Serve with Horseradish Cream, Chili Corn Sauce or New Orleans Barbecue Sauce.

HORSERADISH CREAM

INGREDIENTS

4 cups heavy whipping cream
2 tablespoons prepared horseradish
kosher salt and white pepper to taste
1 tablespoon butter, chilled,
    chopped

■ *Makes 2 cups*

Cook the cream in a heavy saucepot over medium-high heat for 30 minutes or until reduced by 1/2, stirring frequently to avoid scorching. Stir in the horseradish, kosher salt and white pepper. Simmer for 5 to 7 minutes. Whisk in the butter one piece at a time.

Our customers tell us that we have the best fried oysters in town. What's the secret? First, we start with a great product. We've been buying our oysters from the Sunseri family at P&J Oysters for more than fifty years. Second, we know that frying is more than just a cooking method: it's an art. Frying can be done really well, or absolutely horribly. At Palace Café, we've perfected the art of frying oysters. We dust our oysters with a blend of flour, masa for a hint of corn flavor, Creole seasoning for spice and cornstarch so that the oysters fry really crisp. We've also included some of our favorite dipping sauce recipes.

CHILI CORN SAUCE

INGREDIENTS

1 tablespoon chopped garlic
2 tablespoons butter
2 cups fresh corn kernels
1 cup finely chopped red onion
1 cup mixed finely chopped red,
    green and yellow bell peppers
1 cup sliced leeks
1 tablespoon chili powder
2 teaspoons Creole seasoning
2 cups chicken stock (page 197) or
    canned chicken broth
2 cups heavy whipping cream
kosher salt and cracked black
    pepper to taste

■ *Makes 6 to 7 cups*

Sauté the garlic lightly in the butter in a large saucepot. Add the corn, onion, bell peppers, leeks, chili powder and Creole seasoning; mix well. Cook over low heat until the vegetables are tender.

Add the chicken stock and cook for 15 minutes or until the stock is reduced by $1/2$. Stir in the cream and cook until the mixture is reduced by $1/2$ again.

Process half the sauce in a food processor until smooth. Combine with remaining sauce in the saucepot. Season with kosher salt and cracked pepper and cook until heated through.

NEW ORLEANS BARBECUE SAUCE

INGREDIENTS

1 teaspoon chopped garlic
1 tablespoon butter
2 teaspoons cracked black pepper
2 teaspoons Creole seasoning
3 tablespoons Worcestershire sauce
1 tablespoon Crystal hot sauce
juice of 1 lemon
1 cup Abita Amber beer
1 cup (2 sticks) butter, chilled,
    chopped
1 teaspoon minced fresh rosemary

■ *Makes 2$1/2$ cups*

Sauté the garlic lightly in the butter in a medium sauté pan. Increase the heat to high and add the pepper, Creole seasoning, Worcestershire sauce, hot sauce and lemon juice; mix well.

Add the beer, stirring to deglaze the sauté pan. Cook until reduced by $1/2$. Reduce the heat to medium. Add the butter one piece at a time, cooking until the butter melts after each addition and stirring constantly; the sauce should thicken enough to coat the spoon. Stir in the rosemary.

OYSTER PAN ROAST

INGREDIENTS

4 (2- to 3-inch) diagonally sliced
    pieces of French bread
1 tablespoon butter, softened
salt and pepper to taste
1 quart (4 cups) heavy cream
1 tablespoon minced fresh rosemary
1 tablespoon minced shallots
20 freshly shucked oysters
white pepper to taste
1/4 cup bread crumbs
2 tablespoons freshly grated
    Parmesan cheese
4 fresh rosemary sprigs
1 tablespoon finely chopped parsley

■ *Serves 4*

Spread both sides of the French bread pieces with the butter and sprinkle with salt and pepper. Place on a baking sheet and toast at 350 degrees until crisp.

Cook the cream in a heavy saucepot over medium-high heat until reduced by 1/2. Stir in the minced rosemary and shallots. Cook until the sauce is slightly thickened.

Strain the mixture into an ovenproof skillet and bring to a boil. Add the oysters and season with salt and white pepper; do not oversalt as the oysters are somewhat salty. Cook for 1 to 2 minutes or until the edges of the oysters begin to curl.

Mix the bread crumbs and Parmesan cheese in a small bowl and sprinkle the mixture over the oysters. Broil at 350 degrees until the topping is golden brown.

Place one toasted French bread crouton in the center of each of 4 serving plates and spoon the oyster mixture around the croutons. Spear a rosemary sprig through each crouton and sprinkle with parsley.

At Palace Café we serve this signature dish in individual four-ounce French pans, but it's just as good served family-style in a cast-iron skillet.

OYSTER SHOOTERS

SHOOTER SAUCE

4 egg yolks
1 tablespoon dry mustard
1/2 cup red wine vinegar
2 cups vegetable oil
1/4 cup minced shallots
1 teaspoon kosher salt
1 teaspoon coarse pepper

COCKTAIL SAUCE

2 cups ketchup
3 tablespoons prepared horseradish
1 tablespoon Tabasco sauce or other
   hot pepper sauce
juice of 2 lemons

OYSTER SHOOTERS

chilled shot glasses
4 dozen freshly shucked oysters
1/4 cup chopped fresh parsley
2 lemons, thinly sliced

■ *Makes 4 dozen*

Photograph for this recipe is on page 59.

FOR THE SHOOTER SAUCE, combine the egg yolks, dry mustard and wine vinegar in a food processor and process for 30 seconds to blend well. Add the vegetable oil gradually, processing constantly. Add the shallots, salt and pepper and mix well. You may thin the sauce with water if necessary for the desired consistency.

FOR THE COCKTAIL SAUCE, combine the ketchup, horseradish, Tabasco sauce and lemon juice in a mixing bowl and whisk until smooth.

FOR THE OYSTER SHOOTERS, spoon 1 tablespoon of the Shooter Sauce, Cocktail Sauce, or a mixture of both, into each chilled shot glass. Drop 1 oyster into each glass and top it off with a second tablespoon of sauce. Sprinkle each with chopped parsley and garnish with lemon slices.

During the Tennessee Williams Literary Festival, we put these "Oysters in a Glass Menagerie" on the menu and they fly out of the kitchen. They're always a huge hit at parties. Just make big batches of the sauces and chill the beer. The Shooter Sauce is basically a mignonette sauce with a peppery-vinegary taste, that also goes well with all kinds of seafood. To dress them up, top the shooters off with jumbo lump crab meat. If you don't want to contend with all of the shot glasses, serve oysters on the half shell with the sauces on the side.

SEARED SHRIMP BRUSCHETTA WITH CORN AND TOMATO RELISH

CORN AND TOMATO RELISH

1 large Creole tomato
vegetable oil
1 tablespoon chopped garlic
2 tablespoons vegetable oil
1/2 cup fresh corn kernels
1/2 cup finely chopped green bell
    pepper
1/2 cup finely chopped onion
1 tablespoon cane vinegar
1 tablespoon chopped fresh thyme
1/2 cup thinly sliced green onions

SEARED SHRIMP BRUSCHETTA

8 fresh jumbo shrimp, peeled,
    deveined
1/4 cup vegetable oil
1 tablespoon chopped garlic
1 tablespoon Creole seasoning
1 tablespoon butter, softened
4 (1/2-inch) slices Onion Bread
    (page 49)
1 1/2 cups shredded pepper jack
    cheese

GARNISH

4 fresh thyme sprigs
8 pickled okra

■ *Serves 4*

FOR THE RELISH, core the tomato, cut into halves and rub the skin with a small amount of vegetable oil. Make a small slit in the skin of each half and place cut side down on a baking sheet. Roast at 400 degrees until the skins blister. Cool, remove the skins, squeeze out the seeds and chop the tomato.

Sauté the garlic in 2 tablespoons vegetable oil in a large preheated sauté pan until golden brown. Add the corn, green pepper, onion and tomato. Sauté over high heat for 5 to 10 minutes or until the vegetables are tender. Stir in the cane vinegar and fresh thyme. Remove from the heat and let stand for 5 to 10 minutes. Stir in the green onions and cool to room temperature.

FOR THE BRUSCHETTA, make a 1/4-inch-deep cut lengthwise down the back of each shrimp and press the shrimp open by running your thumb down the length of the cut. Whisk the vegetable oil, garlic and Creole seasoning in a bowl. Add the shrimp and marinate in the refrigerator for 1 hour or longer; drain.

Spread the butter on both sides of the Onion Bread and place on a preheated grill pan. Cook just until the bread is marked on both sides. Top each slice with cheese and place on a baking sheet. Bake at 350 degrees for 5 to 10 minutes or until the cheese melts.

Preheat a seasoned cast-iron skillet and add the shrimp. Cook until seared on all sides. Place 2 shrimp on each slice of toast. Serve on the Corn and Tomato Relish and garnish with a sprig of fresh thyme and pickled okra.

For a slightly sweeter taste, add one tablespoon molasses to the marinade. Try substituting mozzarella, Port Salut, provolone or Muenster cheese for the pepper jack cheese.

SEARED GULF SHRIMP WITH CORN GRIT CAKES AND SHRIMP BUTTER

CORN GRIT CAKES

1 tablespoon butter
1/2 cup fresh corn kernels
1/2 cup mixed finely chopped green
    and red bell peppers
1/2 cup finely chopped onion
1 teaspoon Creole seasoning
3 cups water, chicken stock
    (page 197) or canned
    chicken broth
1 cup uncooked white grits
1 tablespoon chopped fresh thyme
kosher salt to taste

SHRIMP BUTTER

reserved heads and tails of
    2 pounds shrimp
2 tablespoons butter
1 teaspoon paprika
1 teaspoon Creole seasoning
1 cup finely chopped onion
1 tablespoon chopped garlic
4 bay leaves
6 black peppercorns
1/2 cup brandy
1/2 cup heavy whipping cream
3 tablespoons chopped fresh
    tarragon
2 cups (4 sticks) butter, chilled,
    chopped

FOR THE GRIT CAKES, melt the butter in a medium saucepot and add the corn, bell peppers, onion and Creole seasoning. Sauté until the vegetables are tender. Add the water and bring to a boil. Stir in the grits and fresh thyme.

Cook over medium heat for 10 to 20 minutes or until thickened, stirring occasionally. Season with kosher salt and keep warm until serving time.

FOR THE BUTTER, sauté the reserved shrimp heads and tails in 2 tablespoons butter in a saucepot over medium heat for 5 to 10 minutes. Stir in the paprika, Creole seasoning, onion, garlic, bay leaves and peppercorns. Cook for 5 to 7 minutes longer, pressing the shrimp heads with a wooden spoon to release the flavorful juices.

Add the brandy and ignite; stir constantly until the flames subside. Stir in the whipping cream and tarragon. Reduce the heat to low and whisk in the chilled butter a few pieces at a time, adding additional butter only after the previous addition has been incorporated. Strain through a fine strainer into a clean saucepot; keep warm until serving time.

SHRIMP

2 pounds (16- to 20-count) fresh
    shrimp
1/4 cup vegetable oil
1 tablespoon chopped garlic
1 tablespoon Creole seasoning
vegetable oil

GARNISH

1 large leek
3 tablespoons all-purpose flour
1 to 2 teaspoons Creole seasoning
vegetable oil for frying
1/4 cup chopped fresh parsley

■ *Serves 6*

FOR THE SHRIMP, peel and devein the shrimp, leaving the tails intact; reserve the heads and shells. Make a 1/4-inch-deep cut down the center of each shrimp and press open by running your thumb down the length of the cut. Whisk 1/4 cup vegetable oil, garlic and Creole seasoning in a bowl. Add the shrimp and marinate for 1 hour or longer.

Add a small amount of additional vegetable oil to the skillet and heat. Drain the shrimp and add to the skillet. Sear on all sides.

To serve, pack the grits tightly into six 4-ounce stainless steel rings. Place on serving plates and carefully remove the rings. Spoon the Shrimp Butter around the cakes and arrange 3 shrimp around each cake with the tails resting on top of the cake.

Cut the leek into 3-inch pieces and then julienne. Place in a bowl of ice water for 5 minutes; drain. Mix the flour with the Creole seasoning and coat the leek with the mixture. Heat vegetable oil in a skillet over high heat and add the leeks. Fry until crisp and golden brown; drain on paper towels. Arrange over the shrimp and grit cakes and top with the chopped parsley.

The key to this recipe is the freshness of the ingredients, especially the shrimp. The sauce is easy to make, extremely flavorful and makes a beautiful, elegant and colorful presentation. You can substitute yellow grits for the white grits, but adjust for the longer cooking time that's required and add a little more liquid if necessary.

SHRIMP REMOULADE

REMOULADE SAUCE

1/4 cup yellow mustard
1/2 cup Creole mustard
1/2 cup ketchup
1/4 cup white vinegar
1/4 cup prepared horseradish
2 eggs
1/4 cup Worcestershire sauce
1 tablespoon hot pepper sauce
2 ribs celery, finely chopped
3 sprigs of parsley, finely chopped
1/2 tablespoon chopped garlic
1/4 bunch green onions, chopped
1/4 lemon, seeded
1/2 tablespoon paprika
1 bay leaf
3/4 cup vegetable oil
salt to taste

SHRIMP AND TOMATOES

3 large Creole tomatoes
2 cups flour
1/4 cup Creole seasoning
4 eggs
2 cups milk
2 cups seasoned bread crumbs
vegetable oil for deep-frying
1 pound (16- to 20-count) shrimp,
    boiled in shrimp boil (page 201)
1 head green leaf lettuce,
    thinly shredded
5 leaves radicchio, thinly shredded
1 carrot, julienned
1/4 cup Fresh Herb Vinaigrette
    (page 108)

GARNISH

2 hard-boiled eggs, chopped
1/2 medium red onion, shaved
6 fresh parsley sprigs

■ *Serves 6*

FOR THE REMOULADE SAUCE, combine the yellow mustard, Creole mustard, ketchup, vinegar, horseradish, eggs, Worcestershire sauce and pepper sauce in a blender. Add the celery, parsley, garlic, green onions, lemon, paprika and bay leaf. Process until smooth. Add the vegetable oil gradually, processing constantly until smooth. Season with salt. Chill until serving time.

FOR THE SHRIMP AND TOMATOES, core the tomatoes and cut into halves crosswise. Scoop out the seeds and pulp with a spoon to create cups. Mix the flour and Creole seasoning in a bowl. Beat the eggs with the milk in a bowl. Place the seasoned bread crumbs in a bowl. Coat each tomato cup with the flour mixture and dip into the egg wash. Repeat the process to double-batter the cups, then coat inside and out with the bread crumbs.

Pour enough vegetable oil to cover the tomato cups completely into a deep saucepot and heat to 350 degrees. Deep-fry the tomato cups for 5 to 7 minutes or until golden brown. Remove with a slotted spoon and place cut side down on paper towels to drain.

Peel and devein the shrimp. Toss the lettuce, radicchio and carrot with the Fresh Herb Vinaigrette in a bowl. Spoon onto the serving plates and place a tomato cup in the center. Fill the cups with Remoulade Sauce and arrange the shrimp tail side out around the edge. Garnish with the boiled eggs, red onion and parsley.

Shrimp Remoulade works well as an appetizer at brunch, lunch or dinner, or as an entrée salad if you throw in a few more shrimp. Shrimp Remoulade is an old New Orleans classic that we thought could be taken to another level, so we've done it a little differently and made it a whole lot better. The flavors of the fried tomato cup and the remoulade sauce really complement each other. The hot tomato cup brings the shrimp to room temperature. The flavor of boiled shrimp changes according to their temperature, and we think room-temperature boiled shrimp taste best.

SEAFOOD BEIGNETS WITH
CREOLE TOMATO TARTAR SAUCE

CREOLE TOMATO TARTAR SAUCE

1 or 2 large Creole tomatoes
1 tablespoon vegetable oil
2 cups mayonnaise
1/4 cup Creole mustard
1/2 cup thinly sliced green onions
1/4 cup finely chopped red onion
juice of 1/2 lemon
1/2 tablespoon horseradish
1/2 tablespoon chopped fresh
    tarragon
1 teaspoon Creole seasoning
hot sauce to taste

SEAFOOD BEIGNETS

31/2 cups all-purpose flour
1 tablespoon baking powder
2 tablespoons Creole seasoning
1/2 cup fresh corn kernels
1/2 cup finely chopped red onion
1/2 cup mixed chopped red, green
    and yellow bell peppers
1/2 cup sliced green onions
1 bottle Abita Amber beer
1/4 cup water
3 eggs
1 cup chopped fresh fish
1 cup chopped shrimp or
    rock shrimp
1 cup crabmeat
vegetable oil for frying

■ *Makes about 50 beignets*

FOR THE TARTAR SAUCE, core the tomatoes and cut into halves. Rub the skins with the vegetable oil and make a small slit in the skin of each half. Place cut side down on a baking sheet and bake at 400 degrees for 15 minutes or until the skins blister. Cool and remove the skins. Squeeze out the seeds and chop.

Combine the tomatoes with the mayonnaise, Creole mustard, green onions, red onion, lemon juice, horseradish, tarragon, Creole seasoning and hot sauce to taste in a large mixing bowl and mix well.

FOR THE BEIGNETS, whisk the flour, baking powder and Creole seasoning in a large mixing bowl. Add the corn, red onion, bell peppers and green onions and mix well. Add the beer, water and eggs and whisk to combine. Fold in the fish, shrimp and crabmeat.

Heat vegetable oil to 350 degrees in a large skillet. Use 2 tablespoons to drop the batter for a few test beignets into the oil, pushing the batter from one spoon with the other inverted spoon. Fry for 5 to 10 minutes or until golden brown and cooked through. Break the beignets open to test for doneness and oil temperature. Adjust the temperature if necessary and fry the remaining beignets. Drain on paper towels. Serve with the tartar sauce for dipping.

Try using different types or combinations of seasonal seafood in the batter to find what you like best. Crawfish, shrimp, crabmeat and light firm fish all work well. Also, try grilling the corn with the husks on before shucking it for beignets with a tad more sweetness.

WILD MUSHROOM CRÊPES

WILD MUSHROOM FILLING

1 pound mixed wild mushrooms,
    such as oyster, button, shiitake
    and crimini
2 tablespoons vegetable oil
1 teaspoon kosher salt
1 teaspoon cracked black pepper
1/2 cup finely chopped shallots
1 teaspoon chopped garlic
2 tablespoons butter
1/4 cup brandy
6 ounces cream cheese, softened
1 teaspoon finely chopped fresh
    rosemary
1 tablespoon finely chopped chives

GRUYÈRE SAUCE

2 cups cream
1 cup shredded Gruyère cheese
2 egg yolks, beaten
kosher salt and white pepper to taste

CRÊPES

16 to 18 crêpes (page 37;
    omit the herbs)
butter

GARNISH

freshly chopped chives
shaved Gruyère cheese

■ *Serves 8 to 10*

FOR THE FILLING, slice the mushrooms into bite-size pieces. Toss the mushrooms with the vegetable oil, kosher salt and cracked pepper in a bowl. Spread on a small baking sheet and roast at 350 degrees for 10 to 12 minutes or until the mushrooms begin to dry. Cool to room temperature.

Sauté the shallots and garlic in the melted butter in a large sauté pan for 10 minutes or until tender. Add the roasted mushrooms and sauté until the liquid has evaporated.

Add the brandy and ignite; failure to ignite indicates that too much liquid remains in the mushrooms. Cook until the flame subsides or until the liquid has evaporated. Fold in the cream cheese, rosemary and chives.

FOR THE SAUCE, bring the cream to a boil in a double boiler or small saucepan. Add the cheese and cook until melted, whisking constantly. Reduce the heat to medium. Whisk a small amount of the warm cream sauce into the egg yolks; whisk the egg yolks into the warm cream sauce. Season with kosher salt and white pepper. Strain into a clean saucepan and keep warm over low heat; do not scorch.

FOR THE CRÊPES, spoon the mushroom filling onto the centers of each crêpe and fold in half or roll to enclose the filling. Melt 1 tablespoon of butter at a time in a skillet over medium-high heat and heat the crêpes in batches in the skillet until warmed through.

To serve, spoon the sauce onto serving plates. Place the crêpes in the sauce. Garnish with the chopped chives and Gruyère cheese.

Wild Mushroom Crêpes is a great dish for dinner parties. It's easy to make, and both the crêpe batter and the filling can be made ahead of time and chilled for up to 12 hours: just stir the crêpe batter well before cooking. You may arrange the crêpes in a baking dish and heat at 350 degrees for 5 to 7 minutes or until warmed through if you prefer. Use the crêpe recipe on page 37, but omit the optional herbs in that recipe. For meatier crêpes, reduce the amount of mushrooms and add some tasso to the filling.

MOLASSES SAUSAGE

INGREDIENTS

2 pounds pork butt, ground
2 teaspoons kosher salt
1/2 teaspoon cracked black pepper
1 teaspoon red pepper flakes
1/2 cup coarsely chopped onion
1/4 cup each coarsely chopped
    celery and bell pepper
2 tablespoons coarsely chopped
    garlic
1 cup thinly sliced green onions
2/3 cup molasses
vegetable oil

■ *Makes 3¹/₂ pounds*

Combine the pork with the kosher salt, cracked pepper and red pepper flakes in a bowl and mix well. Chop the onion, celery, bell pepper and garlic fine in a food processor. Add the pork and pulse until well mixed, adding a couple of ice cubes if necessary to keep the mixture cold. Combine with the green onions and molasses in a large bowl and mix well. Chill, covered, for 1 hour.

Sauté about 1 tablespoon of the sausage mixture in a small amount of vegetable oil in a nonstick skillet to test the flavor. Adjust the seasonings if necessary. Shape into patties and sauté until light brown and cooked through. You may also pipe the mixture into casings and store in the refrigerator for 4 to 5 days or freeze for longer storage.

MUSHROOM SAUSAGE

INGREDIENTS

3 to 4 pounds mixed wild
    mushrooms, such as button,
    crimini and shiitake, thinly sliced
1/2 cup vegetable oil
kosher salt to taste
cracked black pepper to taste
2 pounds pork butt, ground
2 teaspoons kosher salt
1/2 teaspoon cracked black pepper
1 teaspoon red pepper flakes
1/2 cup coarsely chopped onion
1/4 cup each coarsely chopped
    celery and chopped bell pepper
2 tablespoons chopped garlic
1 cup thinly sliced green onions
1/4 cup mixed finely chopped
    thyme, oregano and/or basil
vegetable oil

■ *Makes 3¹/₂ pounds*

Preheat the oven to 350 degrees. Toss the mushrooms with 1/2 cup vegetable oil and kosher salt and cracked pepper to taste in a bowl. Spread evenly on a baking sheet and roast for 10 minutes or until the mushrooms begin to dry; cool.

Combine the pork with 2 teaspoons kosher salt, 1/2 teaspoon cracked pepper and red pepper flakes in a bowl and mix well.

Chop the onion, celery, bell pepper and garlic fine in a food processor. Add the pork and pulse until well mixed, adding a couple of ice cubes if necessary to keep the mixture cold. Combine with the mushrooms, green onions and herbs in a large bowl and mix gently. Chill, covered, for 1 hour.

Sauté about 1 tablespoon of the sausage mixture in a small amount of vegetable oil in a nonstick skillet to test the flavor. Adjust the seasonings if necessary. Shape into patties and sauté until light brown and cooked through. You may also pipe the mixture into casings and store in the refrigerator for 4 to 5 days or freeze for longer storage.

SEAFOOD SAUSAGE

INGREDIENTS

2¹/2 tablespoons minced shallots
1 tablespoon vegetable oil
¹/2 cup thinly sliced green onions
¹/4 cup chopped fresh tarragon
2 pounds firm white fish, such as
    mahi-mahi, redfish, trout, drum or
    sheephead, coarsely chopped
2¹/2 teaspoons kosher salt
1 teaspoon white pepper
¹/8 teaspoon cayenne pepper
2 teaspoons red pepper flakes
¹/2 cup heavy cream
3 egg whites, beaten to soft peaks
vegetable oil

■ *Makes 3¹/2 pounds*

Sauté the shallots in 1 tablespoon vegetable oil in a skillet over medium heat until transparent. Add the green onions and sauté for 1 minute longer. Remove from the heat and stir in the tarragon. Cool to room temperature.

Grind the fish using the grinder attachment on a standing mixer or the smallest die on a meat grinder. Add the kosher salt, white pepper, cayenne pepper and red pepper flakes and process to mix. Add the shallot mixture and mix well. Add the cream gradually, processing constantly until well mixed.

Remove to a large mixing bowl and fold in the egg whites. Chill, covered, in the refrigerator for 1 hour.

Wrap about 1 tablespoon of the sausage mixture tightly in plastic wrap and place in a saucepan of water. Poach the sausage by heating the water gradually to about 140 to 160 degrees. Remove immediately and place in ice water to stop the cooking process; sausage will become gritty and oily if it gets too hot. Taste the sausage and adjust the seasonings.

Shape the sausage into patties and sauté in a small amount of vegetable oil in a nonstick skillet just until cooked through. You may also pipe the sausage mixture into casings and store in the refrigerator for 3 to 4 days.

Making sausage is not difficult. Be careful to keep the sausage mixture cold as it's being mixed in the food processor to prevent it from becoming mushy. If the mixture begins to warm, add a couple of ice cubes while processing, but don't add enough to make the mixture watery. These sausages are great to throw on the grill for po-boys, mixed grills or to serve with egg dishes, in cassoulet or soup.

SMOKED RABBIT RAGOÛT WITH SKILLET CORNBREAD

SMOKED RABBIT STOCK

bones of 1 (3- to 4-pound) smoked
    rabbit
1 tablespoon minced garlic
1 cup finely chopped onion
1 cup finely chopped celery
1 cup finely chopped carrots
6 tablespoons chopped fresh thyme
4 bay leaves
6 black peppercorns
3 quarts (12 cups) water

RAGOÛT

chopped meat of 1 (3- to 4-pound)
    smoked rabbit
1 tablespoon butter
3 cups mixed sliced wild mushrooms
1 cup thinly sliced leeks
1/2 cup finely chopped carrots
1/2 cup fresh English peas or frozen
    green peas
2 tablespoons brandy
2 cups smoked rabbit stock
1/2 cup (1 stick) butter, chilled,
    chopped
kosher salt and cracked black
    pepper to taste
2 tablespoons chopped fresh parsley
1 teaspoon chopped fresh rosemary
1/2 cup thinly sliced green onions
4 radicchio leaves, very thinly sliced
Skillet Cornbread (page 48)

■ *Serves 4*

FOR THE STOCK, combine the rabbit bones with the garlic, onion, celery, carrots, thyme, bay leaves and peppercorns in a large stockpot. Cook until the bones are browned on all sides. Add the water and bring to a boil. Reduce the heat and simmer for 6 hours, skimming the surface. Strain through a fine strainer into a saucepan. Cook over medium heat until reduced to 1 quart. Store unused portion in the refrigerator or freeze for longer storage.

FOR THE RAGOÛT, sauté the rabbit in 1 tablespoon butter in a large sauté pan for 3 to 5 minutes or until light brown. Add the mushrooms, leeks, carrots and English peas and sauté for 3 minutes. Add the brandy, stirring to deglaze the pan. Add the reduced stock and cook until reduced by 1/2.

Whisk in 1/2 cup butter a few pieces at a time, adding additional butter only after the previous addition has been incorporated. Season with kosher salt and cracked pepper. Stir in the parsley, rosemary, green onions and radicchio just before serving to retain the body and color of the radicchio. Ladle into bowls and serve with thick slices of hot cornbread.

To enhance the smoky flavor of the ragoût even more, add some chopped andouille sausage. If you don't like rabbit, substitute smoked chicken. To smoke either the rabbit or chicken, cook it in a home smoker or a grill over wood chips with the top closed. Note that the rabbit stock will need to be made in advance.

GRILLED QUAIL WITH POTATO PANCAKES AND FIVE-PEPPER JELLY

FIVE-PEPPER JELLY

2 cups light corn syrup
2 cups white vinegar
grated zest of 1 lemon
1 teaspoon crushed red pepper
1 1/2 teaspoons finely chopped
    seeded jalapeño pepper
1/2 cup each finely chopped red,
    green and yellow bell peppers

QUAIL

4 quail
2 tablespoons vegetable oil
1 teaspoon chopped fresh garlic
1/2 teaspoon chopped fresh thyme
1/2 teaspoon chopped fresh
    oregano
1/2 teaspoon kosher salt
1/2 teaspoon cracked black pepper

POTATO PANCAKES

1 Idaho potato, peeled
1/2 teaspoon kosher salt
2 teaspoons (or more) all-purpose
    flour
1/2 cup sliced leeks
1 egg yolk
1/4 teaspoon cracked black pepper
1/4 cup vegetable oil

GARNISH

12 to 16 leaves frisée

■ *Serves 4*

FOR THE JELLY, combine the corn syrup, vinegar and lemon zest in a saucepot and cook over high heat for 1 hour or until the mixture is reduced by 1/2 and will coat a spoon. Stir in the crushed red pepper, jalapeño pepper and bell peppers. Simmer over low heat for 10 to 15 minutes or until of the desired consistency. Cool to room temperature. Store in the refrigerator.

FOR THE QUAIL, partially debone the quail, removing the rib bones but leaving the leg bones. Combine the vegetable oil, garlic, thyme, oregano, kosher salt and cracked pepper in a bowl and mix well. Add the quail and marinate, covered, in the refrigerator for 1 hour or longer.

Preheat the grill. Drain the quail and place on the grill. Grill until marked on the skin side and turn a quarter turn to mark again in a diamond pattern. Turn the quail over and grill to medium or until done to taste.

FOR THE PANCAKES, julienne the potato with a mandolin or grate with a grater or in a food processor. Sprinkle with kosher salt and let stand for 5 minutes. Place in a fine strainer and drain to remove the moisture.

Combine the potato, flour, leeks, egg yolk and cracked pepper in a mixing bowl and mix well. Shape lightly into 4 pancakes, adding additional flour if needed to bind.

Heat the vegetable oil in a sauté pan over medium-high heat. Sauté the potato pancakes in the oil until golden brown on both sides. Remove the pancakes from the oil if the oil becomes too hot and the pancakes begin to cook unevenly; finish in a 350-degree oven.

To serve, place a potato pancake on each of 4 serving plates and top with a garnish of frisée. Place the grilled quail on the frisée and drizzle with the pepper jelly.

The Five-Pepper Jelly served with this dish can be made in advance. You may want to wear kitchen gloves while chopping the jalapeño peppers to keep the hot capsaicin from the peppers off your skin.

SMOTHERED DUCK CRÊPE CAKE

ROASTED DUCK

1 (4- to 5-pound) duckling
2 bay leaves
1 sprig of fresh rosemary
1/4 cup finely chopped carrot
1/4 cup finely chopped onion
1/4 cup finely chopped celery
1/2 garlic clove
1/4 cup equal parts kosher salt and
    cracked black pepper
1 cup soy sauce

DUCK SAUCE

reserved duck carcass
1 cup coarsely chopped celery
1 cup coarsely chopped onion
1 cup coarsely chopped carrot
4 bay leaves
6 to 8 black peppercorns
1/4 cup chopped fresh rosemary
1 cup brandy
1/2 cup tomato paste
8 cups water
1/2 cup molasses
2 tablespoons butter, chilled,
    chopped
kosher salt and cracked black
    pepper to taste

TO ROAST THE DUCK, remove the neck and giblets from the duck and reserve them for another use. Rinse the duck well with cold water. Stuff the cavity with the bay leaves, rosemary, carrot, onion, celery and garlic. Season the outside with the mixture of kosher salt and cracked pepper.

Cut a 2- to 3-foot piece of twine. Place the middle of the twine around the remaining portion of the duck's neck. Wrap the ends in an X behind the duck and over the wings, pulling it tight. Pull the ends through the natural creases of the duck's legs; wrap the feet and tie tightly. Chill, covered, for 24 hours.

Preheat the oven to 475 degrees. Rub the duck with the soy sauce and place on the center oven rack; place a baking pan on the rack below the duck to catch the drippings. Roast for 20 minutes. Reduce the oven temperature to 400 degrees and roast for 15 minutes longer or until the duck is cooked medium.

Let stand until cool. Remove the meat from the carcass and reserve both the meat and the carcass.

FOR THE DUCK SAUCE, cut the reserved duck carcass into several small pieces. Brown the bones on all sides in a saucepot over medium-high heat. Add the celery, onion, carrot, bay leaves, peppercorns and rosemary. Cook for 10 to 15 minutes or until the vegetables are tender, stirring frequently. Add the brandy, stirring to deglaze the skillet.

Stir in the tomato paste and cook over medium heat for 10 minutes. Add the water and bring to a boil. Reduce the heat and simmer for 1 to 1 1/2 hours, skimming and discarding the oil and impurities that collect on the surface as needed.

Strain the stock and return to the saucepan. Stir in the molasses and cook for 20 minutes or until slightly thickened. Whisk in the butter gradually. Season with kosher salt and cracked pepper.

SMOTHERED DUCK CRÊPES

1 tablespoon chopped garlic
1 tablespoon butter
3 cups chopped roasted duck meat
1 1/2 cups half-moon leek slices
1 1/2 cups fresh corn kernels
1 tablespoon chili powder
1 1/2 cups duck sauce
1 teaspoon chopped fresh rosemary
1 teaspoon chopped fresh oregano
1 teaspoon chopped fresh parsley
1 cup chopped roasted red pepper
1 cup chopped green onions
kosher salt and cracked pepper
    to taste
5 or 6 crêpes (page 37;
    omit the herbs)

■ *Serves 6 to 8*

This smothered Duck Crêpe Cake is not difficult, but it's time consuming. You may want to roast the duck and make the duck sauce, filling and crêpe batter the day before. Then all you'll have to do is make the crêpes and assemble the cake before serving it. You may even assemble the cake earlier in the day on the day it's to be served and refrigerate it until time to bake. But note, the cake can become mushy if assembled too early. The dish can also be served as individual smothered duck crêpes. Try enhancing the crêpe batter with a tablespoon of a chopped fresh herb such as oregano.

FOR THE CRÊPES, sauté the garlic in the butter in a saucepot over medium heat. Add the reserved duck meat and sauté until light brown. Add the leeks, corn and chili powder and cook until the vegetables are tender. Stir in the duck sauce and cook over medium heat for 20 minutes, stirring occasionally to coat the meat well. Add the rosemary, oregano, parsley, roasted red pepper and green onions. Season with kosher salt and cracked pepper. Let stand until cool.

To assemble, preheat the oven to 350 degrees and spray a baking sheet with nonstick cooking spray. Place one crêpe on the baking sheet and spread the filling mixture about 1/4 inch thick over the crêpe. Repeat the process to make a cake 5 or 6 layers high. Bake for 8 to 12 minutes. Let stand for 5 minutes, then slice into wedges. Spoon the remaining warmed duck sauce onto the serving plates and place a cake wedge on each plate.

SOUPS · SALADS

STOCKPOTS ARE BRIMMING AND READY TO FORM THE BASIS FOR

THE SOUPS. THE PACE IN THE KITCHEN PICKS UP UNTIL IT'S IN FULL

SWING. METAL POTS CLANG AS THEY MEET STAINLESS STEEL

COUNTERS, AND THE AROMAS OF PURPLE ONION AND BLEU CHEESE

FROM THE SALAD STATION MELD. BRIGHT RED STRAWBERRIES

FROM PONCHATOULA CONTRAST WITH THE DARK GREEN OF

SPINACH. A TOUCH OF DRESSING, AND THE DISH IS PERFECTION.

GRAND CHEFS SERIES AT THE GRAND HOTEL

Fairhope, Alabama

This event began as a single vintner dinner with Palace Café and Mondavi wines. It has since grown into a series of four weekends featuring foods from various family restaurants, including Dickie Brennan's Palace Café and Dickie Brennan's Steakhouse. Each of the weekends, spread throughout the summer months, includes cooking demonstrations, wine tastings and a gala dinner for more than 100 people.

MENU

Robert Mondavi Coastal Chardonnay, 1998
Robert Mondavi Coastal Merlot, 1997

Blue Crab Soft-Shell Bisque
with a Spicy Fried Crab Cake
Robert Mondavi Fume Blanc, 1998

Duck Confit Salad with Foie Gras Vinaigrette
and Shaved Truffle Cheese
Byron Pinot Noir, 1997

Petit Filet Mignon served on
Smoked Onion Mashed Potatoes with
a Brandy Cream Sauce and Wild Mushrooms
Robert Mondavi Cabernet Sauvignon, 1996

Chocolate Chocolate Cake
served with Praline Ice Cream
and Chocolate and Caramel Sauces

WEST VIRGINIA'S CANCER CENTER 10TH ANNIVERSARY GALA

White Sulphur Springs, West Virginia

In April of 1995, West Virginia's Cancer Center held its 10th Anniversary Gala.

Palace Café considers it an honor to have been invited, along with

Cakebread Cellars, to provide the meal for the evening. It's always a welcome

opportunity to return to West Virginia, where the event was held, and to

see the friends we've made there over the years.

MENU

Creole Onion Soup with Aged Cheddar
Sauvignon Blanc, Cakebread Cellars, Napa Valley, 1993

Grilled Redfish served on a bed of Maque Choux
with a Lemon Butter Sauce
Chardonnay, Cakebread Cellars, Napa Valley, 1993

Sazerac Sorbet

Tournedos of Beef with Louisiana Crabmeat
and Choron Sauce
Cabernet Sauvignon, Rutherford Reserve, Cakebread Cellars, Napa Valley, 1989

White Chocolate Bread Pudding

Coffee and Cordials

RED BEAN SOUP

INGREDIENTS

2 pounds dried red beans
1 cup (2 sticks) butter
4 ounces andouille sausage or
    smoked sausage
2 meaty ham hocks, or 4 ounces
    chopped ham
2 cups chopped celery
2 cups chopped onion
2 cups chopped green bell pepper
2 tablespoons chopped garlic
1 tablespoon finely chopped fresh
    thyme
4 bay leaves
2 tablespoons Creole seasoning
2 gallons chicken stock (page 197)
    or canned chicken broth
1 cup (2 sticks) butter, chilled,
    chopped

■ *Serves 28 as an appetizer or
18 as an entrée*

Sort and rinse the dried beans. Combine the beans with enough water to cover in a large bowl and soak for 8 hours or longer; drain.

Melt the 1 cup butter in a large saucepot and add the sausage and ham hocks. Cook until brown on all sides. Add the celery, onion, bell pepper, garlic, thyme, bay leaves and Creole seasoning. Cook for 10 to 20 minutes or until the vegetables are tender.

Add the red beans and chicken stock. Bring to a boil and reduce the heat. Simmer for 45 to 60 minutes or until the beans are tender. Remove the ham hocks and discard the bay leaves.

Cool the ham hocks enough to handle. Remove the meat from the bones and add to the soup. Purée the soup in batches in a food processor and return to the saucepot. Simmer over low heat until thick enough to coat the spoon. Whisk in the chopped butter a few pieces at a time to thicken the soup and enhance the flavor. Ladle soup into bowls and serve.

Monday is traditionally Red Beans and Rice day in New Orleans. We serve Red Beans on Mondays for "family meal," along with fried chicken, salad and cornbread. What better way to start a shift!

Red Bean Soup is a variation on the same theme. If you slowly cook it down with a few extra ham hocks, it also makes a great party dip to serve with gaufrette potatoes or potato chips (page 54).

FIVE-ONION SOUP

INGREDIENTS

1 cup (2 sticks) butter
3 Vidalia onions, julienned
3 red onions, julienned
1 bunch leeks, julienned
5 shallots, julienned
1 bottle Abita Amber beer
8 cups chicken stock (page 197) or
    canned chicken broth
1 pint heavy cream
kosher salt and white pepper to taste

GARNISH

1 cup freshly chopped chives

■ *Serves 12 as an appetizer or*
8 as an entrée

Melt the butter in a large saucepot over medium heat. Add the Vidalia onions, red onions, leeks and shallots. Cook, covered, over low heat for 30 minutes or until the onions are tender and begin to release their natural sugars. Add the beer, stirring to deglaze the saucepot.

Add the chicken stock and bring to a boil. Reduce the heat and simmer for 20 minutes or until the soup is reduced by 1/4. Stir in the cream and season with kosher salt and white pepper. Purée the soup in batches and return to the saucepot.

Simmer for 10 to 15 minutes or until heated through. Ladle into soup bowls and garnish with the chives.

We also like Five-Onion Soup served in the classic French style, topped with rustic French bread croutons and melted Gruyère or Swiss cheese.

We think there are few things finer than cooking with Creole tomatoes during the summer, but meaty beefsteak tomatoes are a good substitute when Creoles can't be found. Creole Tomato Soup, a big green salad and some hot crusty bread make a great summertime lunch or dinner. We also like the thought of curling up with a big bowl of this soup and a grilled cheese sandwich on a lazy afternoon.

Pictured in the photograph clockwise from top right are Blue Crab Soft-Shell Bisque (page 95), Creole Tomato Basil Soup and Sweet Potato and Andouille Soup.

90

CREOLE TOMATO BASIL SOUP

INGREDIENTS

4 pounds Creole tomatoes
1/2 cup (1 stick) butter
3 cups chopped onions
2 cups chopped celery
1 tablespoon chopped garlic
1/2 cup tomato paste
1 cup dry vermouth
8 cups chicken stock (page 197) or
    canned chicken broth
1 cup heavy cream
1 tablespoon Creole seasoning
1 tablespoon sugar
1 cup thinly sliced fresh basil
kosher salt and cracked black
    pepper to taste

■ *Serves 20 as an appetizer or
12 as an entrée*

Preheat the oven to 400 degrees. Core the tomatoes and cut into halves. Score the skin with a sharp knife and place cut side down on a baking sheet. Roast for 15 minutes or until the skins blister. Cool and remove the skins. Squeeze the tomatoes over a strainer into a bowl to remove the seeds; reserve the strained juice and tomatoes.

Melt the butter in a large saucepot. Add the onions, celery and garlic. Cook, covered, over low heat until tender. Add the tomatoes and tomato paste. Cook for 10 to 15 minutes.

Add the vermouth and stir to deglaze the saucepot. Stir in the chicken stock and bring to a boil. Reduce the heat to a simmer and stir in the cream, Creole seasoning and sugar.

Purée in batches in a food processor and return to the saucepot. Add the basil and simmer for 10 to 15 minutes or until heated through and of the desired consistency. Season with kosher salt and cracked pepper.

SWEET POTATO AND ANDOUILLE SOUP

INGREDIENTS

5 pounds sweet potatoes
1/2 cup (1 stick) butter
1 pound andouille sausage, sliced
1 cup finely chopped celery
1 cup finely chopped onion
3 quarts (12 cups) chicken stock
    (page 197) or canned
    chicken broth
1/2 cup molasses
kosher salt and white pepper to taste

■ *Serves 20 as an appetizer or
12 as an entrée*

Place the whole unpeeled sweet potatoes in a baking pan and bake at 350 degrees for 1 hour or until easily pierced with a knife and the sugars begin to be released. Cool, peel and chop the sweet potatoes.

Melt the butter in a large saucepot and add the sausage. Cook until the sausage is brown. Add the celery and onion and sauté for 10 to 15 minutes or until tender. Add the sweet potatoes and chicken stock. Bring to a boil and reduce the heat. Simmer for 5 to 10 minutes or until the flavors blend.

Purée the soup in batches in a food processor. Return to the saucepot and stir in the molasses, kosher salt and white pepper. Simmer for 10 minutes or until heated through. Serve with thick slices of Skillet Cornbread (page 48) or hush puppies.

CHICKEN AND ANDOUILLE GUMBO

INGREDIENTS

1 (3 1/2- to 4-pound) chicken
1 tablespoon (or more) Creole
   seasoning
vegetable oil for browning the
   chicken
2/3 cup vegetable oil
1 cup all-purpose flour
3 cups chopped celery
3 cups chopped onions
3 cups chopped bell peppers
1/4 cup chopped garlic
1 pound andouille sausage, sliced
6 bay leaves
1 cup tomato paste
1 teaspoon chili powder
1 gallon chicken stock (page 197)
   or canned chicken broth
1/2 cup chopped fresh oregano
salt and pepper to taste
cooked Louisiana long grain
   white rice

GARNISH

2 cups chopped green onions

■ *Serves 24 as a appetizer or
16 as an entrée*

Cut the chicken into 8 pieces and season on all sides with the Creole seasoning. Heat just enough vegetable oil to cover the bottom of a large saucepot over high heat. Add the chicken and cook until brown on all sides. Remove to paper towels to drain.

Add 2/3 cup vegetable oil to the saucepot and heat over high heat until hot but not smoking. Whisk in the flour gradually. Cook until the roux is amber in color, whisking constantly.

Add the celery, onions, bell peppers and garlic. Cook for 10 minutes or until the vegetables are tender; the roux will cool down with the addition of the vegetables, which will release their natural sugars causing the roux to darken.

Stir in the andouille, bay leaves, tomato paste and chili powder. Cook for 5 to 10 minutes, stirring constantly. Stir in the chicken stock and bring to a boil. Reduce the heat and simmer for 30 minutes, skimming the surface.

Add the chicken pieces or boned chicken and oregano and simmer for 30 minutes longer. Season with salt and pepper and serve over hot cooked Louisiana long grain white rice. Garnish with the green onions.

We use a dark roux made with oil rather than with butter for gumbo, because oil has a higher smoking point than butter, which burns easily.
You may add the chicken pieces skin and all to the gumbo as they do in the country, or debone the chicken, chop it and add it to the gumbo. It's a matter of preference.

CORN AND CRAB SOUP

INGREDIENTS

2 cups (4 sticks) butter
4 cups all-purpose flour
1/2 cup (1 stick) butter
2 cups finely chopped celery
2 cups finely chopped onions
2 cups finely chopped leeks
2 cups fresh corn kernels
3 bay leaves
1 gallon crab stock (page 196)
1 quart (4 cups) heavy cream
2 tablespoons finely chopped
    fresh thyme
1 pound lump crabmeat
2 cups chopped green onions
kosher salt and white pepper to taste

■ *Serves 24 as an appetizer or
16 as an entrée*

Melt 2 cups butter in a saucepot over medium heat and whisk in the flour. Cook for 10 to 15 minutes or until the roux is golden brown, or blond, whisking constantly; remove from the heat.

Melt 1/2 cup butter in a large saucepan over medium heat. Add the celery, onions, leeks, corn and bay leaves. Sauté for 10 to 15 minutes or until the vegetables are tender. Add the crab stock and bring to a boil.

Whisk a small amount of the hot soup into the roux, then whisk the roux into the hot soup. Reduce the heat and simmer for 20 to 30 minutes, skimming the surface. Stir in the cream and thyme and simmer for 10 minutes. Add the crabmeat and green onions. Season with kosher salt and white pepper and simmer for 10 to 15 minutes or until of the desired consistency. Remove the bay leaves before serving.

resh local ingredients, corn cut right off the cob and beautiful lump crabmeat make this soup a year-round favorite with our local guests.

BLUE CRAB SOFT-SHELL BISQUE

INGREDIENTS

1 cup (2 sticks) butter
2 cups all-purpose flour
2 tablespoons butter
2 cups finely chopped carrots
2 cups finely chopped onions
2 cups finely chopped celery
1 tablespoon chopped garlic
6 bay leaves
6 soft-shell crabs, cleaned
1/2 cup tomato paste
3 tablespoons finely chopped
    fresh thyme
3 tablespoons finely chopped
    fresh tarragon
1 cup brandy
1 gallon crab stock (page 196)
2 cups heavy cream
1 teaspoon saffron
salt and white pepper to taste

■ *Serves 30 as an appetizer or
20 as an entrée*

*Photograph for this recipe is on
page 90.*

Melt 1 cup butter in a small saucepot and gradually whisk in the flour. Cook for 10 to 15 minutes or until the roux is golden brown, or blond, whisking constantly; remove from the heat.

Melt 2 tablespoons butter in a large saucepot and add the carrots, onions, celery, garlic and bay leaves. Cook, covered, over low heat for 15 to 20 minutes or until tender. Add the crabs, tomato paste, thyme and tarragon. Cook for 5 to 10 minutes or until heated through.

Stir in the brandy and cook for 5 minutes. Add the crab stock and bring to a boil. Whisk a small amount of the hot soup into the roux, then whisk the roux into the hot soup. Reduce the heat and simmer for 30 to 45 minutes or until of the desired consistency, skimming the surface.

Purée with an immersion blender or in batches in a food processor. Strain through a fine strainer into the saucepot. Bring to a simmer over low heat. Stir in the cream and saffron and season with salt and white pepper. Simmer for 15 minutes over low heat.

Serve rich Blue Crab Soft-Shell Bisque as an appetizer or an entrée. It's delicious ladled over crab cakes or garnished with jumbo lump crabmeat and fried or marinated crab claws.

We use blue crabs for this bisque. To clean soft-shell crabs, cut straight across about 1/4 inch below the eyes with sharp kitchen shears and remove the head portion. Turn the crabs on their backs and open the shell flaps. Remove the stringy gray lungs, which we refer to as "dead men," and the stomach, or "sand sack."

OYSTER AND EGGPLANT SOUP

INGREDIENTS

2 cups (4 sticks) butter
4 cups all-purpose flour
1/2 cup (1 stick) butter
2 pounds eggplant, peeled, chopped
1 pound leeks, sliced into half-moon pieces
1 pint oysters
1 gallon chicken stock (page 197) or canned chicken broth
1 cup heavy cream
1/4 cup Worcestershire sauce
1 tablespoon finely chopped fresh oregano
1 tablespoon finely chopped fresh thyme
1 tablespoon Creole seasoning
kosher salt and white pepper to taste

GARNISH

1 cup sliced green onions

■ *Serves 24 as an appetizer or 16 as an entrée*

Melt 2 cups butter in a small saucepan over medium heat and gradually whisk in the flour. Cook for 10 to 15 minutes or until the roux is golden brown, or blond, whisking constantly; remove from the heat.

Melt 1/2 cup butter in a large saucepot over medium-high heat. Add the eggplant and leeks and cook, covered, for 15 to 20 minutes or until tender.

Drain the oysters, reserving 1/2 cup liquid. Add the reserved liquid and chicken stock to the soup. Bring to a boil. Whisk a small amount of the hot soup into the roux, then whisk the roux into the hot soup. Reduce the heat.

Stir in the cream, Worcestershire sauce, oregano, thyme and oysters. Season with the Creole seasoning, kosher salt and white pepper. Bring just to a simmer.

Purée the soup with an immersion blender or in small batches in a food processor. Garnish servings with the sliced green onions.

We purée the oysters in this recipe for a smooth flavorful soup, but you may also add a few more whole oysters to the soup just before serving.

OYSTER DOME SOUP

INGREDIENTS

1/2 cup (1 stick) butter
1 cup all-purpose flour
1 tablespoon butter
2 cups finely chopped celery
2 cups finely chopped onions
1 tablespoon finely chopped
    fresh thyme
6 bay leaves
1 tablespoon chopped garlic
6 cups (or more) chicken stock
    (page 197) or canned
    chicken broth
6 dozen oysters
1 cup heavy cream
2 cups chopped green onions
kosher salt and white pepper to taste
2 sheets frozen puff pastry, thawed
2 eggs
1/2 cup milk

■ *Serves 12*

Melt 1/2 cup butter in a small saucepot over medium heat and whisk in the flour gradually. Cook for 10 to 15 minutes or until the roux is golden brown, or blond, whisking constantly; remove from the heat.

Melt 1 tablespoon butter in a large saucepan and add the celery, onions, thyme, bay leaves and garlic. Sauté over medium heat until tender. Stir in 6 cups chicken stock.

Drain the oysters, reserving the liquid. Add enough additional chicken stock to the reserved liquid to measure 2 cups. Stir into the soup and bring to a boil. Whisk a small amount of the hot soup into the roux, then whisk the roux into the hot soup. Simmer for 35 to 45 minutes. Stir in the cream and green onions; season with kosher salt and white pepper. Simmer for 10 minutes longer. Cool to room temperature; discard the bay leaves.

Place 6 oysters in each of 12 small baking dishes or ramekins. Ladle the soup into the dishes. Cut 12 rounds of puff pastry 1/2 inch larger than the tops of the dishes. Place on the dishes and press to the edges of the bowls.

Beat the eggs with the milk in a small bowl. Brush over the pastry. Bake at 375 degrees for 20 to 25 minutes or until the puff pastry rises to form a dome and is golden brown.

This is a great soup with a beautiful and elegant presentation to serve at dinner parties. The puff pastry seals in the heat so the soup stays hot longer. Keep an eye on the soup in the oven and adjust the oven temperature if the pastry appears to be cooking too quickly or too slowly.

SEAFOOD GUMBO

INGREDIENTS

1 cup vegetable oil
1 cup all-purpose flour
4 cups chopped celery
4 cups chopped onions
4 cups chopped bell peppers
1/4 cup chopped garlic
1 tablespoon chopped fresh thyme
8 bay leaves
1 cup tomato paste
1 teaspoon cayenne pepper
1 1/2 gallons crab stock (page 196)
2 cups chopped tomatoes
1 pound okra, sliced
3 large blue crabs
1 pound (36- to 40-count) shrimp,
    boiled, peeled
2 cups chopped green onions
1/2 cup Worcestershire sauce
salt to taste
2 dozen freshly shucked oysters
steamed white rice

■ *Serves 8 to 12*

Heat the oil in a large saucepot over medium-high heat until hot but not smoking. Whisk in the flour gradually. Cook for 20 minutes or until the roux is a dark amber color, whisking rapidly.

Add the celery, onions and bell peppers. Cook for 10 to 20 minutes or until the vegetables are tender; the roux will cool slightly as the vegetables are added and darken as the vegetables release their natural sugars. Stir in the garlic, thyme, bay leaves, tomato paste and cayenne pepper. Cook for 5 to 10 minutes or until heated through, stirring occasionally.

Add the crab stock and tomatoes. Bring to a boil and reduce the heat to medium. Simmer for 5 to 10 minutes, skimming the surface. Add the okra and crabs and simmer for 30 minutes. Add the shrimp, green onions and Worcestershire sauce. Season sparingly with salt, allowing for the saltiness of the oysters.

Simmer for 20 minutes, continuing to skim the surface. Add the oysters just before serving and simmer just until the edges begin to curl. Discard the bay leaves and serve over steamed white rice.

The key to making a great gumbo, or any other soup, is to use a good stock. You can also add some andouille or smoked sausage to enhance the flavor if you like. Serve the gumbo in a large bowl with hot French bread, butter and cold beer!

Remember that the darker the roux, the thinner the gumbo, because when you cook a roux, the gluten is cooking out of the flour. If you burn your roux, throw it out and begin again; a burned roux will make the gumbo taste bitter.

TURTLE SOUP

INGREDIENTS

1 cup (2 sticks) butter
1 1/2 cups all-purpose flour
3 medium onions, coarsely chopped
8 ribs celery, coarsely chopped
4 bell peppers, coarsely chopped
2 tablespoons blend of 80%
    vegetable oil and 20% olive oil
2 pounds turtle meat, ground
1/4 cup chopped garlic
1 tablespoon chopped fresh thyme
2 cups tomato purée
1 cup Worcestershire sauce
1 cup Crystal hot sauce
1 1/2 gallons veal stock (page 199)
1 lemon
8 ounces fresh spinach, chopped
4 hard-boiled eggs, chopped
1 cup sherry
kosher salt and freshly ground
    pepper to taste

■ *Serves 8 to 12*

Melt the butter in a small saucepan over medium heat and whisk in the flour gradually. Cook for 10 to 15 minutes or until the roux is golden brown, or blond, whisking constantly; remove from the heat.

Purée the onions, celery and bell peppers in a food processor. Heat the oil blend in a large saucepot over medium heat and add the turtle meat. Cook until brown; drain the saucepot and return to the heat. Add the puréed vegetables, garlic, thyme, tomato purée, Worcestershire sauce and hot sauce; mix well. Simmer for 20 minutes.

Add the veal stock and bring to a boil; reduce the heat to medium. Whisk a small amount of the hot soup into the roux, then whisk the roux into the hot soup. Cook for 30 to 40 minutes, stirring occasionally and skimming the surface.

Purée the lemon in a food processor. Stir the lemon, spinach and chopped eggs into the soup and cook for 20 to 30 minutes or until the soup is of the desired consistency. Stir in the sherry and season with kosher salt and freshly ground pepper.

Although the turtle meat that we use today is farm-raised, years ago the turtles came straight from the bayous. Turtle soup was a staple of the Creoles and the buccaneers of the Caribbean as well, because turtle meat was so readily available and always fresh. Today, turtle soup is to most New Orleanians what chicken soup is to the rest of the country.

DUCK CONFIT SALAD WITH FOIE GRAS VINAIGRETTE

FOIE GRAS VINAIGRETTE

4 ounces foie gras
1/4 cup finely chopped shallots
1 teaspoon dry mustard
1 teaspoon cracked black pepper
1 cup blend of 80% vegetable oil
    and 20% olive oil
1/2 cup rice wine vinegar
salt to taste

DUCK CONFIT AND CRACKLINGS

2 bay leaves
1 small bunch fresh thyme
1/2 cup kosher salt
1/2 cup cracked black pepper
2 legs of 1 (4- to 5-pound) Maple
    Leaf duck
2 cups blend of 80% vegetable oil
    and 20% olive oil or rendered
    duck fat
2 garlic cloves, chopped
1 tablespoon soy sauce

SALAD

8 ounces mixed baby greens
1/4 cup shaved red onion
1/2 cup julienned carrot
1/2 cup fresh blueberries
1/2 cup fresh raspberries

■ *Serves 4*

FOR THE VINAIGRETTE, chop the foie gras into small pieces and sear in a small skillet; drain, reserving the foie gras and the drippings. Combine the drippings, shallots, dry mustard and cracked pepper in a large stainless steel bowl. Whisk in the oil blend gradually. Whisk in the vinegar. Stir in the foie gras and season with salt.

FOR THE CONFIT AND CRACKLINGS, grind the bay leaves, thyme, 1/2 cup salt and 1/2 cup cracked pepper in a food processor. Rub the duck legs with the mixture. Refrigerate, covered, for 24 hours.

Preheat the oven to 200 to 225 degrees. Combine the oil blend and garlic in a baking dish and warm in the oven. Wipe the rub off the duck legs and place in the baking dish. Roast for 45 to 60 minutes or until cooked through and tender. Remove the duck from the baking dish. Cool to room temperature. Remove the meat from the bones, reserving the skin for cracklings.

Season the reserved duck skin with the soy sauce and kosher salt and cracked pepper to taste. Place in a baking pan and bake at 350 degrees until partially cooked. Remove from the baking pan and cool, reserving the pan drippings. Julienne the duck skin. Fry in the reserved drippings in a skillet until crisp; drain.

FOR THE SALAD, combine the greens, red onion, carrot and 1 cup of the Duck Confit in a large bowl. Add the desired amount of Fois Gras Vinaigrette and toss to coat well.

To serve, spoon the salad onto 4 serving plates. Sprinkle the blueberries and raspberries over and around the salad and top with 1/2 cup of the Duck Cracklings.

CRABMEAT RAVIGOTE

RAVIGOTE SAUCE

2 cups mayonnaise
1/4 cup Creole mustard
1 teaspoon Crystal hot sauce
1 teaspoon Worcestershire sauce
juice of 1 lemon
1/4 cup chopped capers
1/4 cup horseradish
1/4 cup minced red onion

CRABMEAT RAVIGOTE

1 pound jumbo lump crabmeat
kosher salt and cracked black
    pepper to taste
4 Creole tomatoes, thickly sliced
1/2 head green leaf lettuce, very
    thinly sliced

GARNISH

1/4 cup capers
1 lemon, sliced into wheel shapes

■ *Serves 4*

FOR THE SAUCE, combine the mayonnaise, Creole mustard, hot sauce, Worcestershire sauce and lemon juice in a mixing bowl or food processor and mix until smooth. Add the capers, horseradish and red onion and mix well. Store in the refrigerator.

FOR THE CRABMEAT, sprinkle the crabmeat with kosher salt and cracked black pepper. Combine with 1/4 cup of the sauce in a bowl and toss gently; do not break up the crabmeat.

Place 3 slices of tomato in a circle on each of 4 serving plates. Place the lettuce in the center of each plate and top with the crabmeat mixture. Garnish with the capers and lemon wheels.

The sauce used as a dressing in Crabmeat Ravigote is a Creole favorite that's also good with grilled or baked fish, boiled or fried shrimp, fried eggplant and other dishes.

CREAMY BLEU CHEESE DRESSING

2 cups sour cream
1/2 cup buttermilk
1 tablespoon Worcestershire sauce
1 teaspoon Crystal hot sauce
juice of 1/2 lemon
juice of 1/2 lime
1/2 cup finely chopped onion
2 cups crumbled bleu cheese
1 teaspoon cracked black pepper

FOR THE DRESSING, combine the sour cream, buttermilk, Worcestershire sauce, hot sauce, lemon juice and lime juice in a mixing bowl and whisk until smooth. Add the onion and bleu cheese and season with the cracked pepper; mix well. Store in the refrigerator for up to 2 weeks.

HERB CROUTONS

1 cup French bread cubes
blend of 80% vegetable oil and 20% olive oil
dried thyme and oregano to taste

FOR THE CROUTONS, toss the bread cubes with a small amount of oil blend and thyme and oregano to taste in a bowl. Spread on a baking sheet and bake at 325 to 350 degrees until dry and crisp.

SALAD

1 head romaine
kosher salt and cracked black pepper to taste
1/4 cup shaved red onion
1 cup crumbled bleu cheese

FOR THE SALAD, tear the lettuce into bite-size pieces. Season with kosher salt and cracked pepper. Toss with 1/2 cup of the dressing in a bowl. Spoon onto 4 serving plates and top with the onion, bleu cheese and croutons.

■ *Serves 4*

A few tips for salads: Always rinse greens and vegetables in ice water to keep them crisp. . . . Dry greens completely, as dressings, especially creamy dressings, won't stick to wet greens. . . . Tear greens or use a very sharp knife to cut them; greens chopped with dull knives will bruise and discolor.

We always make more salad dressing than we need. Homemade dressings are always great to have on hand, and most taste better a few days after you make them. Just be sure to store them properly and to whisk or shake them well before each use.

FRISÉE SALAD WITH WARM PHYLLO-WRAPPED GOAT CHEESE

WALNUT VINAIGRETTE

1/4 cup finely chopped shallots
1 tablespoon dry mustard
1 teaspoon sugar
1/4 cup Champagne vinegar
1 cup walnut oil

FRISÉE SALAD

4 phyllo sheets
1/4 cup clarified butter
4 ounces goat cheese
16 ounces frisée
1/4 cup shaved red onion
4 ounces bacon, crisp-fried,
    chopped
salt and pepper to taste

■ *Serves 4*

FOR THE VINAIGRETTE, combine the shallots, dry mustard, sugar and vinegar in a bowl or food processor. Whisk or process until smooth. Whisk or blend in the walnut oil gradually. Store in the refrigerator.

FOR THE SALAD, brush the sheets of phyllo with the clarified butter and fold each sheet into a 4-inch-wide strip. Place 1/4 of the goat cheese near the end of each strip and fold over several times to make rectangular pockets.

Brush both sides of the phyllo-wrapped pockets with the clarified butter and sauté in a nonstick skillet until golden brown on both sides.

Combine the frisée with the red onion, bacon and 1/2 cup of the Walnut Vinaigrette in a bowl and toss to coat well. Season with salt and pepper. Spoon onto 4 serving plates and top each with a goat cheese pocket.

To clarify the butter for the Phyllo-Wrapped Goat Cheese, melt unsalted butter in a small saucepan over low heat. Skim and discard any foam from the surface and pour the clear golden butter off the milk solids, which will have settled to the bottom.

MAYTAG AND
SPICED PECAN SALAD

MAYTAG VINAIGRETTE

1/4 cup finely chopped shallots
1/2 cup red wine vinegar
1/4 cup Worcestershire sauce
1/4 cup Crystal hot sauce
1/2 teaspoon cracked black pepper
2 cups blend of 80% vegetable oil
    and 20% olive oil
1/2 cup crumbled Maytag bleu
    cheese
kosher salt to taste

SPICED PECANS

1/4 cup pecans
1/2 tablespoon butter, melted
1/4 tablespoon Creole seasoning
sugar to taste

SALAD

16 ounces mixed baby greens
kosher salt and cracked black
    pepper to taste
1/4 cup juilienned carrot
1/4 cup shaved red onion
1/2 cup crumbled bleu cheese
1 cup Herb Croutons (page 103)

■ *Serves 4 to 6*

FOR THE VINAIGRETTE, combine the shallots, red wine vinegar, Worcestershire sauce, hot sauce and cracked pepper in a mixing bowl. Whisk in the oil blend gradually.

Whisk in the bleu cheese and season with kosher salt, adjusting the amount of salt according to the strength and flavor of the bleu cheese. Store in the refrigerator for up to 2 weeks.

FOR THE SPICED PECANS, preheat the oven to 325 degrees. Toss the pecans with the melted butter, Creole seasoning and sugar in a bowl, coating well. Spread the pecans on a baking sheet and toast for 5 to 8 minutes or until light brown.

FOR THE SALAD, season the greens with kosher salt and cracked pepper in a bowl. Add the carrot, red onion and 1/4 cup of the vinaigrette and toss lightly.

Spoon onto serving plates and top with the bleu cheese, Herb Croutons and pecans.

Maytag bleu cheese can be hard to find. Danish bleu cheese makes a good substitute in this dressing, but Stilton will overpower the other flavors. For a creamier dressing, add half of the bleu cheese and blend the dressing with an immersion blender or in a food processor, then whisk in the remaining bleu cheese.

CAFÉ SPINACH SALAD

PECAN VINAIGRETTE

2 cups pecans
3 cups blend of 80% vegetable oil
    and 20% olive oil
1 cup molasses
2/3 cup cane vinegar, champagne
    vinegar or apple cider vinegar
1 teaspoon cracked black pepper
kosher salt to taste

SPICED PECANS

1/2 cup pecans
1 tablespoon butter, melted
1/2 tablespoon Creole seasoning
sugar to taste

SALAD

16 ounces fresh spinach, stems
    removed
kosher salt and cracked black
    pepper to taste
1/4 cup shaved red onion
1/2 cup crumbled ricotta cheese

■ *Serves 4*

FOR THE VINAIGRETTE, combine the pecans and oil blend in a saucepan. Cook, covered, over medium heat for 15 to 20 minutes or until the natural oil of the pecans is released, stirring occasionally. Cool to room temperature.

Whisk in the molasses, cane vinegar and cracked pepper. Season with kosher salt. Store in the refrigerator for up to several weeks.

FOR THE PECANS, preheat the oven to 325 degrees. Toss the pecans with the melted butter, Creole seasoning and sugar in a bowl, coating well. Spread on a baking sheet and toast for 5 to 8 minutes or until light brown.

FOR THE SALAD, sprinkle the spinach with kosher salt and cracked pepper in a bowl. Add 1/2 cup of the vinaigrette and toss to coat well. Spoon onto serving plates and top with the red onion, spiced pecans and ricotta cheese.

We like ricotta cheese in our Café Spinach Salad. Hard mild cheeses, like Pecorino Romano, that won't overpower the other flavors in the salad, or even a hard goat cheese, can be substituted.

PONCHATOULA STRAWBERRY AND SPINACH SALAD

BALSAMIC VINAIGRETTE

3 tablespoons finely chopped shallots
1 tablespoon sugar
1/2 cup balsamic vinegar
1 teaspoon kosher salt
1 teaspoon cracked black pepper
2 cups blend of 80% vegetable oil and 20% olive oil

SALAD

1 pint Louisiana strawberries, stemmed, cut into quarters
16 ounces fresh spinach
kosher salt and cracked black pepper to taste
1/4 cup shaved red onion
1/2 cup crumbled ricotta salata cheese

■ *Serves 4*

Photograph for this recipe is on page 97.

FOR THE VINAIGRETTE, combine the shallots, sugar, balsamic vinegar, kosher salt and cracked pepper in a large bowl or food processor and whisk or process until smooth. Whisk or blend in the oil gradually. Store in the refrigerator for up to several weeks.

FOR THE SALAD, combine the strawberries and spinach in a large bowl and season with kosher salt and cracked pepper. Add 1/3 cup of the vinaigrette and toss gently. Spoon onto salad plates and top with the red onion and ricotta salata cheese.

The sweetest strawberries anywhere are grown right here in Louisiana, and Ponchatoula is one of the largest producers. Bright red all the way through the berry, Ponchatoula strawberries have almost double the sugar content of the average strawberry. Just take a visit to the Ponchatoula Strawberry Festival held each spring if you don't believe us. You should, however, use the freshest local produce that's available to you.

CREOLE TOMATO SALAD

FRESH HERB VINAIGRETTE

1 cup Champagne vinegar or rice
    wine vinegar
1 teaspoon dry mustard
1/2 cup finely chopped shallots
1 teaspoon sugar
1 teaspoon cracked black pepper
3 cups blend of 80% vegetable oil
    and 20% olive oil
1 cup chopped fresh herbs, equal
    parts basil, thyme, tarragon,
    chives and oregano
kosher salt to taste

SALAD

1/2 bunch watercress
4 medium Creole tomatoes
kosher salt and cracked black
    pepper to taste
6 ounces fresh mozzarella or other
    soft cheese, cut into 4 slices
1 Vidalia onion, shaved or thinly
    sliced

■ *Serves 4*

FOR THE VINAIGRETTE, combine the vinegar, dry mustard, shallots, sugar and cracked pepper in a large mixing bowl or food processor and whisk or process to mix well. Whisk or blend in the oil blend very gradually. Whisk in the fresh herbs and season with kosher salt.

FOR THE SALAD, cut off the watercress stems about 1/2 inch below the leaves and discard the stems. Arrange several sprigs of watercress on each serving plate. Slice each tomato into 1-inch slices, discarding the stem and blossom ends. Season with kosher salt and cracked pepper.

Layer 1 slice of tomato, a slice of mozzarella cheese and a second slice of tomato on each prepared plate. Top with the Vidalia onion and drizzle with 1/4 cup of the vinaigrette.

During the hottest summer months, no lunch or dinner is complete without a simple salad of thickly sliced Plaquemine Parish Creole tomatoes, fresh mozzarella cheese and sweet Vidalia onions. You can vary this classic salad by adding a chiffonnade of fresh basil and rustic French bread croutons, or by drizzling it with other dressings, such as Balsamic Vinaigrette (page 107).

The Fresh Herb Vinaigrette is extremely versatile. It's great drizzled over grilled fish, or used as a marinade for steaks.

WERLEIN SALAD

WERLEIN DRESSING

2 eggs
4 anchovies
3 tablespoons red wine vinegar
1/2 tablespoon sugar
1 teaspoon chopped garlic
1 teaspoon chopped shallot
1 teaspoon cracked black pepper
3 cups blend of 80% vegetable oil
    and 20% olive oil

SALAD

1 head romaine
1/2 cup freshly grated Romano
    cheese
salt and cracked black pepper
    to taste

GARNISH

freshly grated Romano cheese
Herb Croutons (page 103)

■ *Serves 4*

FOR THE DRESSING, combine the eggs, anchovies, vinegar, sugar, garlic, shallot and cracked pepper in a food processor and process until well mixed. Add the oil blend gradually, processing constantly until smooth.

FOR THE SALAD, tear the romaine into bite-size pieces. Toss with 1/2 cup Romano cheese, 1/2 cup of the dressing, salt and cracked pepper in a bowl. Spoon onto serving plates. Garnish with additional Romano cheese and croutons.

Sturdier greens like romaine will hold up best when tossed with this creamy Caesar-style dressing, named for the family whose music store once occupied the Café building. Top the salad with grilled chicken, shrimp or flash-fried oysters for a great entrée salad.

SEAFOOD

SOME OF THE MOST FERTILE FISHING GROUNDS ANYWHERE ARE

FOUND WHERE THE MUDDY WATERS OF THE MISSISSIPPI RIVER MEET THE

WARM BLUE WATERS OF THE GULF OF MEXICO. YELLOW FIN TUNA, TROUT,

MAHI MAHI AND COUNTLESS OTHER TYPES OF FISH ARE CAUGHT IN THE

EARLY MORNING AND DELIVERED TO OUR RECEIVING DOOR BEFORE

NOON. SACKS OF OYSTERS ARRIVE, DESTINED TO BE SERVED WITH PASTA,

IN COURT-BOUILLION, OR MAYBE FRIED. AND FROM OUR BAYOUS COME

THE CRAWFISH, A LOUISIANA STAPLE, AND ALLIGATOR, THE NEWEST

ADDITION TO THE MENU.

STONE CRAB AND SEAFOOD FESTIVAL

Longboat Key, Florida

The annual celebration of the deliciously sweet stone crab is a party from start to finish at The Colony Beach and Tennis Resort in Longboat Key, Florida. Palace Café and Dickie Brennan teamed up with Tony Mantuano of Chicago's Tuttaposto restaurant to create one of the courses for the weekend. For the lucky attendees, it's a chance to feast on crab prepared in every way imaginable.

MENU

Stone Crab Sausage with Shrimp Bordelaise and Boniato Croquette

Speckled Trout with Rock Shrimp and Roasted Garlic Linguine

Stuffed Quail with a Warm Salad of Red Cabbage,
Duck Confit, Potatoes and Goat Cheese

Grilled Boneless Lamb Chops with
Wild Cherry Ginger Sauce and
Barley Couscous Timbale

Le Trois Friandise

LUNCH FOR THE PRESIDENT

New Orleans, Louisiana

The President of the United States surprised Palace Café when he showed

up for lunch on Thursday, May 30, 1996. The five-course lunch

President Clinton enjoyed confirmed his reputation for having a healthy

appetite. Lunch at Palace Café was the only meal that the President was able to

include in his schedule while he was in New Orleans.

MENU

Marinated Crab Claws

Crawfish Gazpacho

Pan-Seared Yellowfin Tuna
in a Creole Tomato Cream with Crawfish Tails

Catfish Pecan Meunière served with
Green Beans and Rice Pilaf

Raspberry Sorbet
White Chocolate Bread Pudding
Country Apple Pie

CATFISH PECAN MEUNIÈRE

SPICED PECANS

3 cups pecan halves or pieces
2 tablespoons butter, softened
2 tablespoons sugar
2 tablespoons Creole seasoning
2 tablespoons Worcestershire sauce

CREOLE MEUNIÈRE SAUCE

1 lemon, peeled, cut into quarters
1/2 cup Worcestershire sauce
1/2 cup Crystal hot sauce
1/4 cup heavy whipping cream
2 cups (4 sticks) butter, chilled,
    cut into small pieces
kosher salt and white pepper to taste

CATFISH

3 eggs
1 cup milk
1 cup all-purpose flour
6 (5- to 7-ounce) catfish fillets
Creole seasoning to taste
vegetable oil for sautéing

■ *Serves 6*

FOR THE PECANS, combine the pecans with the butter, sugar, Creole seasoning and Worcestershire sauce in a bowl and mix until the pecans are evenly coated. Spread on a baking sheet and toast at 350 degrees for 10 to 15 minutes or until golden brown. Cool to room temperature.

FOR THE SAUCE, combine the lemon, Worcestershire sauce and hot sauce in a heavy saucepot. Cook over medium heat until the liquid is thick and syrupy, whisking constantly. Whisk in the whipping cream and reduce the heat to low.

Add the butter one piece at a time, mixing until the butter has been completely incorporated after each addition. Remove from the heat and stir until smooth. Season with kosher salt and white pepper. Strain through a fine strainer into a saucepot and keep warm.

FOR THE CATFISH, beat the eggs and milk in a mixing bowl. Combine half the spiced pecans with the flour in a food processor and pulse until finely ground. Spread the pecan flour evenly on a flat surface.

Trim the catfish fillets and season on both sides with Creole seasoning. Dip fillets in the egg wash, then press them into the pecan flour to coat well.

Heat vegetable oil in a large skillet or sauté pan until hot but not smoking. Add the catfish fillets and sauté for 4 to 5 minutes or until light brown on the bottom. Turn the fillets with a spatula, taking care not to break the pecan crust, and sauté for 3 to 4 minutes longer or until brown.

To serve, place the catfish fillets on serving plates and top with the sauce and remaining spiced pecans.

This classic New Orleans dish can be prepared with catfish, trout, drum, sheephead, snapper, or any line-caught flaky white fish. We serve our Catfish Pecan Meunière with popcorn rice and steamed vegetables.

REDFISH ON THE HALF SHELL

REDFISH

2 whole (4-pound) redfish
2 tablespoons Creole seasoning
1 red onion, thinly sliced
1 tablespoon vegetable oil
kosher salt and cracked black
    pepper to taste
Lemon Beurre Blanc (page 195)

GARNISH

4 sprigs flat-leaf parsley
2 lemons, cut into 4 crowns

■ *Serves 4*

TO FILLET THE FISH, place it on its side and cut one side from the bone, starting below the head and finishing above the tail, using the backbone to guide the knife. Turn the fish over and cut the second fillet from the backbone. Discard the head, bone and tail. Feel for any remaining bones and remove them with needle-nose pliers.

To cook the fish, preheat the grill to medium-low. Season both sides of the fillets with the Creole seasoning. Place skin side down on the grill and cover loosely with foil. Grill for 5 to 10 minutes or until the fish flakes easily.

Toss the red onion with the vegetable oil, kosher salt and cracked pepper in a bowl. Grill until tender-crisp.

To serve, ladle the Lemon Beurre Blanc onto serving plates. Place one fillet skin side down on each plate and top with the grilled red onion. Garnish with the parsley and lemon crowns.

*R*edfish on the Half Shell has all of the great flavors of roasted whole fish, but it's easier to eat. You can substitute snapper, drum, sheephead or other fish with thick enough scales to hold up on the grill for the redfish. If your market does not have fish with the scales still intact, place the fish skin down on foil instead of directly on the grill.

The sauce is very delicate and can break easily. Be sure to use cold butter and to whisk continuously over medium-low heat while preparing it.

GARLIC-CRUSTED GULF FISH WITH BARBECUE SAUCE

GREEN ONION SALAD

2 bunches green onions
1 teaspoon vegetable oil
1 tablespoon cane vinegar
kosher salt and cracked black
    pepper to taste

YUKON GOLD MASH

1 1/2 pounds Yukon Gold potatoes
1/2 cup (1 stick) butter
1/2 cup warm milk
kosher salt and white pepper to taste

GARLIC-CRUSTED FISH

2 cups all-purpose flour
1/4 cup chopped garlic
2 teaspoons kosher salt
2 teaspoons cracked black pepper
4 (8-ounce) redfish, snapper or drum
    fillets with skin
kosher salt and cracked black
    pepper to taste
4 egg whites, slightly beaten
vegetable oil for sautéeing
New Orleans Barbecue Sauce
    (page 67)

MASA FRIED OYSTERS

1/2 cup masa harina
1/2 cup all-purpose flour
1/4 cup cornstarch
1 tablespoon Creole seasoning
1 pint oysters, drained
vegetable oil for frying

■ *Serves 4*

FOR THE SALAD, cut the green onions into 2-inch pieces then julienne. Combine with ice water in a bowl and let stand for 25 minutes or until the green onions curl.

At serving time, drain the green onions and combine with the oil, vinegar, kosher salt and cracked pepper in a bowl and toss to coat well.

FOR THE MASH, cook the potatoes in enough water to cover in a saucepan for 45 minutes or until tender; drain. Combine with the butter in a large bowl and mash with a large spoon. Add the warm milk, kosher salt and white pepper and mix, leaving the mixture somewhat chunky. Keep warm.

FOR THE FISH, combine the flour, garlic, 2 teaspoons kosher salt and 2 teaspoons cracked pepper in a food processor and pulse to mix well; spread on a work surface. Sprinkle both sides of the fish with additional kosher salt and cracked pepper. Dip in the egg whites and press into the garlic flour, coating well.

Heat oil in a large sauté pan over high heat. Add the fish skin side down and reduce the heat to medium. Cook until golden brown on the bottom. Turn the fish with a spatula and cook until golden brown and flaky.

FOR THE OYSTERS, mix the masa harina, flour, cornstarch and Creole seasoning in a large bowl. Coat the oysters with the flour mixture, shaking off any excess.

Heat vegetable oil to 350 degrees in a skillet. Add one oyster and fry to test the oil temperature; oysters burn easily if the oil is too hot, yet can become greasy if the oil is not hot enough. Fry the remaining oysters in batches until golden brown and hot through to the centers; drain on paper towels. Keep warm.

To serve, spoon the potato mash into the center of each serving plate. Place a fish fillet skin side up on the mash and ladle New Orleans Barbecue Sauce around the fillet. Place the oysters around the fillet and top with the green onion salad.

SPECKLED TROUT WITH ROCK SHRIMP AND GARLIC LINGUINE

SMOKED SHIITAKE SALAD

1 cup shiitake mushroom caps
1 red bell pepper, julienned
2 tablespoons extra-virgin olive oil
1 teaspoon Champagne vinegar
kosher salt and cracked black
    pepper to taste

ROCK SHRIMP AND ROASTED GARLIC LINGUINE

2 tablespoons blend of 80%
    vegetable oil and 20% olive oil
4 ounces rock shrimp, (36- to 40-
    count) shrimp or stone crabmeat
1 cup sliced leeks
1/2 cup roasted garlic (see note)
1/2 cup fish stock (page 199) or
    chicken stock (page 197)
1 cup heavy cream
12 ounces linguine, cooked al dente
1/2 bunch green onions, sliced
2 tablespoons unsalted butter,
    chilled, sliced
kosher salt and cracked black
    pepper to taste

SPECKLED TROUT

4 (7-ounce) speckled trout fillets
1 tablespoon Creole seasoning
1 cup all-purpose flour
1/4 cup blend of 80% vegetable oil
    and 20% olive oil

GARNISH

2 tablespoons truffle oil
4 sprigs of flat-leaf parsley

■ *Serves 4*

FOR THE SALAD, place the mushrooms in a perforated pan, steamer or colander and place over wood chips in a larger saucepan; cover with foil. Smoke over medium-high heat for 30 minutes. The mushrooms can also be smoked over wood chips in a closed grill or home smoker. Julienne the smoked mushroom caps and combine with the bell pepper, olive oil and vinegar in a bowl and toss to mix well. Season with kosher salt and cracked pepper.

FOR THE LINGUINE, heat the oil blend in a large sauté pan. Add the rock shrimp and leeks and sauté until the rock shrimp are partially cooked. Add the roasted garlic, fish stock and cream, stirring to deglaze the sauté pan. Cook until the liquid is reduced by 1/3.

Fold in the pasta and green onions. Cook until the pasta is heated through. Fold in the butter and cook just until the sauce thickens. Season with kosher salt and cracked pepper.

If using stone crabmeat, fold it in along with the pasta and green onions so that it doesn't overcook.

FOR THE TROUT, preheat the oven to 350 degrees. Season the trout fillets on both sides with the Creole seasoning. Coat with flour, shaking off the excess. Heat the oil blend in a large oven-safe sauté pan. Add the trout and sauté until golden brown; cook in 2 batches if necessary to prevent over-crowding. Turn the fillets over and place the sauté pan in the oven. Bake for 5 to 8 minutes or until the fillets flake easily.

To serve, spoon the linguine onto serving plates. Arrange the trout fillets over the linguine. Top with the smoked shiitake salad. Garnish with a drizzle of truffle oil and a sprig of the parsley.

To roast garlic, toss the garlic cloves with a small amount of oil and roast at 350 degrees for 30 to 45 minutes or until golden brown.

ANDOUILLE-CRUSTED FISH WITH CAYENNE BUTTER SAUCE

CHIVE AÏOLI

1/4 cup chopped garlic
2/3 cup blend of 80% vegetable oil
    and 20% olive oil
1 bunch chives
2 tablespoons chopped parsley
2 egg yolks
1 teaspoon Dijon mustard
juice of 1 lemon
salt to taste

CAYENNE BUTTER SAUCE

3/4 cup Crystal hot sauce
1 cup (2 sticks) butter, chopped,
    chilled

ANDOUILLE-CRUSTED FISH

6 ounces andouille sausage or
    smoked pork sausage, coarsely
    chopped
1 onion, coarsely chopped
2 tablespoons blend of 80%
    vegetable oil and 20% olive oil
1 cup bread crumbs
4 (8-ounce) skinless boneless
    fish fillets
kosher salt and white pepper to taste
3 tablespoons blend of 80%
    vegetable oil and 20% olive oil

■ *Serves 4*

FOR THE CHIVE AÏOLI, cook the garlic in the oil blend in a saucepan over medium heat for 20 minutes, stirring frequently; do not brown. Strain into a bowl and cool.

Reserve 8 chive pieces for garnish. Purée the remaining chives and parsley in a food processor. Add the egg yolks and pulse to mix well. Add the garlic oil gradually, processing constantly. Add the Dijon mustard, lemon juice and salt and mix, adding a small amount of water if necessary for a thin mayonnaise-like consistency. Spoon into a pastry tube or plastic squeeze bottle and chill for up to several days.

FOR THE BUTTER SAUCE, cook the hot sauce in a small saucepan over medium heat until reduced by 1/3. Reduce the heat to low and whisk in the butter a few pieces at a time, mixing well after each addition. Keep warm.

FOR THE FISH, grind the andouille in a food processor. Sauté the ground andouille with the onion in 2 tablespoons oil blend in a skillet over medium heat until the sausage is brown and the onion is transparent. Purée the mixture in a food processor. Add the bread crumbs and pulse until mixed.

Preheat the oven to 350 degrees. Season the fish on both sides with kosher salt and white pepper. Heat 3 tablespoons oil blend in an ovenproof skillet over high heat. Add the fish fillets and sear for 2 minutes. Turn the fillets over and drain the skillet. Press the andouille mixture onto the fish to form a crust. Bake for 5 to 10 minutes or until the fish flakes easily and the crust is golden brown.

To serve, ladle the butter sauce onto each serving plate. Place 1 fish fillet on each plate and drizzle the chive aïoli across the fish in a zigzag pattern. Top with the reserved chive pieces.

At Palace Café, we prepare this signature dish with redfish, drum, sheephead, grouper, snapper or catfish, depending on what's fresh and in season. We serve it with haricots verts, carrots and rissolé potatoes.

ANDOUILLE-CRUSTED SOFT-SHELL CRABS WITH CRABMEAT RISOTTO

GREEN PEPPER AÏOLI

1/4 cup chopped green onions,
    puréed
1 tablespoon Tabasco green pepper
    sauce
2 egg yolks
1 1/2 cups blend of 80% vegetable
    oil and 20% olive oil
kosher salt to taste

CRABMEAT RISOTTO

1 cup chopped onion
1/2 cup (1 stick) butter
16 ounces uncooked arborio rice
6 cups crab stock (page 196)
16 ounces jumbo lump crabmeat
1/2 cup very thinly sliced fresh basil
kosher salt and cracked black
    pepper to taste

ROASTED TOMATO SAUCE

3 or 4 medium tomatoes
vegetable oil
1/2 cup Tabasco sauce
2 cups white wine
2 shallots, minced
3/4 cup heavy cream
3 cups (6 sticks) butter, chilled,
    chopped

FOR THE AÏOLI, combine the green onions, green pepper sauce and egg yolks in a food processor and pulse to mix well. Add the oil blend gradually, processing constantly and adding a small amount of water if necessary for a thin mayonnaise-like consistency.

Season with kosher salt and spoon the aïoli into a plastic squeeze bottle.

FOR THE RISOTTO, sauté the onion in the butter in a large saucepot until tender. Add the rice and sauté over low heat for 5 minutes, stirring constantly with a wooden spoon. Bring the crab stock to a simmer in a saucepot.

Add the crab stock to the rice 2 cups at a time, cooking until the crab stock has been absorbed after each addition and stirring frequently for a total of 30 to 45 minutes. Fold in the crabmeat and basil. Season with kosher salt and cracked pepper. Keep warm until serving time.

FOR THE SAUCE, core the tomatoes and cut into halves. Rub the skins with a small amount of oil and make a slit in the skin of each half. Arrange cut side down in a baking pan and roast at 400 degrees until the skins blister. Cool, remove the skins, squeeze out the seeds and chop the tomatoes.

Combine the Tabasco sauce, white wine and shallots in a medium saucepot and cook for 20 minutes or until syrupy. Add the roasted tomatoes and cook until the juices evaporate. Stir in the cream and simmer until the sauce is thick enough to coat the spoon. Reduce the heat to low. Whisk in the butter a few pieces at a time, mixing well after each addition. Keep warm until serving time.

SOFT-SHELL CRABS

10 large soft-shell crabs
1 onion, coarsely chopped
1 1/4 pounds andouille sausage,
    coarsely chopped
2 tablespoons vegetable oil
4 cups bread crumbs
2 cups all-purpose flour
1 tablespoon Creole seasoning
6 eggs
2 cups milk
vegetable oil for frying

■ *Serves 10*

FOR THE CRABS, cut straight across the crabs about 1/4 inch below the eyes with sharp kitchen shears and remove the head portion. Turn the crabs on their backs and open the shell flaps. Remove the stringy gray lungs, which we refer to as "dead men," and the stomach, or "sand sack."

Grind the onion and andouille in a food processor. Sauté in 2 tablespoons vegetable oil in a skillet until brown. Combine with the bread crumbs in a mixing bowl and mix well, adding a small amount of additional oil if necessary to bind the mixture. Mix the flour and Creole seasoning in a bowl. Beat the eggs lightly with the milk in another bowl.

Coat the crabs with the flour mixture and shake off any excess. Dip in the egg wash and press into the andouille mixture, coating well. Heat oil to 350 degrees in a skillet. Place the crabs one at a time over a ladle, allowing the legs to hang off the sides. Deep-fry the legs in the hot oil for 1 to 2 minutes or until cooked and stiff. Turn the crab over and fry the body for 5 to 7 minutes or until cooked through.

To serve, spoon the Crabmeat Risotto onto serving plates and ladle the Roasted Tomato Sauce around the risotto. Place the crabs with the legs up on the risotto and drizzle with the aïoli.

Our guests love our signature Andouille-Crusted Fish (page 118) so much that we decided to try the concept with soft-shell crabs. The andouille, onion and bread crumb mixture adds spice to the dish and fries crispy and brown.

CRABMEAT AU GRATIN

INGREDIENTS

1 1/2 cups heavy cream
4 ounces Port Salut cheese, chopped
4 ounces Romano cheese, grated
1 pound jumbo lump crabmeat
1 cup chopped green onions
kosher salt and cracked black
     pepper to taste
1/2 cup fresh bread crumbs

GARNISH

1 tablespoon minced red bell
     pepper
2 to 4 sprigs of flat-leaf parsley

■ *Serves 2 as an entrée or*
4 as an appetizer

Bring the cream to a boil in a heavy saucepot. Reduce the heat to low and stir in the cheeses. Heat until the cheeses melt, stirring constantly.

Strain the cheese sauce over the crabmeat in a large mixing bowl. Add the green onions, and toss lightly to avoid breaking up the crabmeat. Season with kosher salt and cracked pepper and toss lightly.

Spoon into ramekins and top with the bread crumbs. Bake at 350 degrees for 20 to 25 minutes or until the crabmeat is heated through and the bread crumbs are toasted. Garnish with the red bell pepper and parsley.

You can change the flavor of Crabmeat au Gratin by adding other seafood, such as shrimp, or by using a different blend of cheeses, such as Gruyère or Jarlsberg. Just stay away from any cheese that's too salty or too strong; you need to use a blend of cheeses that will complement, rather than overpower, the sweet taste of the crabmeat.

BARBECUE SHRIMP

INGREDIENTS

1 teaspoon chopped garlic
1 tablespoon butter
1 pound jumbo shrimp
3 tablespoons Worcestershire sauce
1 tablespoon Crystal hot sauce
juice of 1 lemon
2 teaspoons Creole seasoning
2 teaspoons cracked black pepper
1 cup Abita Amber beer
1 cup (2 sticks) butter, chilled,
　　chopped
1 teaspoon minced fresh rosemary
French bread, thickly sliced on the
　　diagonal, warmed

■ *Serves 2*

Sauté the garlic lightly in the butter in a medium sauté pan. Add the shrimp and cook for 1 minute on each side. Increase the heat to high and add the Worcestershire sauce, hot sauce, lemon juice, Creole seasoning and cracked pepper. Add the beer and stir to deglaze the sauté pan. Cook until reduced by $1/2$.

Reduce the heat to medium and add the butter one piece at a time, mixing until completely incorporated after each addition and cooking until the sauce is thickened enough to coat the spoon. Stir in the rosemary. Ladle into bowls. Serve with hot French bread to sop up the sauce.

For a dish that's easy to eat, but still has that classic Barbecue Shrimp presentation, peel the shrimp, leaving the heads and tails on, before adding them to the sauce. Leave the shrimp out, and you have a great New Orleans barbecue sauce recipe. We like to toss fried oysters in this sauce to make barbecue oyster po-boys on hot French bread.

SHRIMP CREOLE

INGREDIENTS

6 Creole tomatoes
vegetable oil
1/2 cup (1 stick) butter
2 cups chopped green bell peppers
2 cups chopped celery
2 cups chopped onions
1 tablespoon chopped garlic
4 bay leaves
1 teaspoon chopped fresh thyme
1/2 cup tomato paste
1/2 teaspoon cayenne pepper
4 cups crab stock (page 196)
1/2 cup light corn syrup
1 tablespoon cane vinegar
1/4 cup cornstarch
3 pounds (16- to 20-count) shrimp,
    peeled, deveined
1 teaspoon crushed red pepper
1 tablespoon vegetable oil
1 cup thinly sliced green onions
1/2 cup chopped fresh basil
kosher salt and cracked black
    pepper to taste

■ *Serves 8*

Core the tomatoes and cut into halves. Rub the skins with a small amount of vegetable oil and cut a small slit in each. Arrange cut side down in a baking pan and roast at 400 degrees for 15 minutes or until the skins blister. Cool the tomatoes, remove the skins, squeeze out the seeds and chop.

Melt the butter in a large saucepot and add the bell peppers, celery, onions, garlic, bay leaves and thyme. Cook until the vegetables are tender. Add the roasted tomatoes, tomato paste and cayenne pepper. Mix well and cook over medium heat for 10 minutes.

Add the stock and bring to a boil. Reduce the heat to a simmer and stir in the corn syrup and cane vinegar. Simmer for 10 minutes. Dissolve the cornstarch in a small amount of water in a small bowl to make a paste or slurry. Temper the slurry into the sauce and simmer for 10 minutes, stirring occasionally and skimming the surface.

Sauté the shrimp with the crushed red pepper in 1 tablespoon vegetable oil in a saucepan until partially cooked. Add the shrimp, green onions and basil to the Creole sauce and simmer for 5 minutes or until the shrimp are cooked through. Discard the bay leaves and season with kosher salt and cracked pepper. Serve with Louisiana Popcorn Rice (page 129) or white rice.

The secret to making great Shrimp Creole is not overcooking the shrimp. Sauté the shrimp until partially cooked, then stir them in at the end. A touch of cane vinegar and basil freshens up the dish and enhances the flavor.

DRUNKEN SHRIMP PASTA

INGREDIENTS

3 tomatoes
1 or 2 red bell peppers
vegetable oil
1 quart (4 cups) heavy whipping
  cream
2 teaspoons chopped garlic
1 tablespoon butter
1 1/2 pounds (16- to 20-count)
  shrimp, peeled, deveined
1 cup sliced leeks
2 cups julienned shiitake mushrooms
1 tablespoon Creole seasoning
1 bottle Abita Amber beer
16 ounces angel hair pasta, cooked
  al dente
kosher salt to taste
1/2 cup freshly grated Romano
  cheese

GARNISH

4 sprigs of flat-leaf parsley

■ *Serves 4*

Core the tomatoes and cut into halves. Core the bell peppers and cut into halves lengthwise, discarding the seeds and membranes. Rub the skins of the tomatoes and bell peppers with a small amount of vegetable oil and make a small slit in the skin of each tomato half. Arrange cut side down in a baking pan and roast at 400 degrees until the skins blister. Cool the tomatoes and bell peppers and remove the skins. Squeeze the seeds from the tomatoes and chop coarsely. Julienne the bell peppers.

Bring the cream to a boil in a heavy saucepot. Stir in the roasted tomatoes and cook until the mixture is reduced by 1/3 and the sauce will coat the spoon.

Sauté the garlic in the butter in a large sauté pan until golden brown. Add the shrimp, leeks, mushrooms and Creole seasoning. Sauté until the shrimp are partially cooked. Add the beer and stir to deglaze the pan. Cook until the beer has evaporated.

Add the tomato cream and pasta; mix well and season with kosher salt. Spoon onto serving plates and top with the Romano cheese and roasted bell peppers. Garnish with the flat-leaf parsley.

We also like this dish made with julienned chicken breast instead of shrimp.

PASTA ST. CHARLES

INGREDIENTS

2 cups heavy cream
2 tablespoons Creole mustard
12 ounces andouille sausage
2 tablespoons butter
16 ounces jumbo shrimp, peeled,
    deveined
2 tablespoons minced garlic
1 teaspoon Creole seasoning
8 ounces penne, cooked al dente
2 tablespoons butter, chilled
kosher salt and cracked black
    pepper to taste

GARNISH

2 bunches green onions, sliced
1/2 cup freshly grated Parmesan
    cheese

■ *Serves 4*

Bring the cream to a boil in a small saucepot and reduce the heat to medium. Cook until reduced by 1/2. Whisk in the Creole mustard and remove from the heat.

Cut the sausage into halves lengthwise and then slice. Sauté in 2 tablespoons butter in a large sauté pan for 1 minute. Add the shrimp, garlic and Creole seasoning. Sauté for 5 minutes or until the shrimp are cooked through.

Stir in the reduced cream sauce. Fold in the pasta and 2 tablespoons chilled butter to richen the sauce. Season with kosher salt and cracked pepper. Garnish servings with the green onions and Parmesan cheese.

Pasta St. Charles, featured regularly on the lunch menu at Palace Café, has become a Mardi Gras parade party favorite. Many parades roll down St. Charles Avenue, which connects the residential area of town to downtown and the French Quarter. Residents host parties and serve huge meals to their guests. This particular dish is a much anticipated part of a Mardi Gras celebration, especially for Lauren Brennan Brower's gathering.

SHRIMP TCHEFUNCTE

LOUISIANA POPCORN RICE

1/2 cup (1 stick) butte
2 cups uncooked popcorn rice
3 cups water

CREOLE MEUNIÈRE SAUCE

3 lemons, peeled, cut into quarters
3 tablespoons Crystal hot sauce
1/2 cup Worcestershire sauce
1/4 cup heavy whipping cream
4 cups (8 sticks) butter, chopped,
    chilled

SHRIMP

1 tablespoon chopped garlic
2 tablespoons butter
2 pounds medium shrimp, peeled,
    deveined
3 cups sliced domestic mushrooms
1 tablespoon Creole seasoning
3 cups chopped green onions

■ *Serves 6*

FOR THE RICE, melt the butter in a medium saucepot and add the rice. Sauté for 2 minutes. Stir in the water. Cook, uncovered, over medium-high heat until the rice has absorbed the water and is tender. Cover and keep warm until serving time.

FOR THE SAUCE, combine the lemons, hot sauce and Worcestershire sauce in a medium saucepot and cook over low heat until reduced by 2/3. Add the whipping cream and cook until reduced by 1/2, whisking constantly. Add the chilled butter a few pieces at a time, mixing constantly until completely incorporated after each addition. Strain through a fine strainer into another saucepot and keep warm.

FOR THE SHRIMP, sauté the garlic in the butter in a large sauté pan until golden brown. Add the shrimp, mushrooms and Creole seasoning. Sauté until the shrimp are 3/4 cooked.

Reserve some of the green onions for garnish. Stir the remaining green onions and the meunière sauce into the shrimp and mushrooms. Cook over low heat until the shrimp are firm and cooked through.

To serve, pack the rice into a shallow cup and invert onto the serving plates; lift carefully. Spoon the shrimp and sauce around the Louisiana Popcorn Rice. Garnish with the reserved green onions.

Named for a local Native American tribe that inhabited this area, the Tchefuncte River is located just north of New Orleans. The part of the tribe that inhabited the coastal area was thought to have enjoyed the same seafood that we love so much today. Shrimp Tchefuncte is a wonderful dish, rich in flavor, that is great for lunch or dinner. We like to dress up this signature dish by using jumbo shrimp and mixed wild mushrooms rather than domestic ones.

FLASH-FRIED BAYOU OYSTERS WITH LINGUINE

INGREDIENTS

1/2 cup (1 stick) butter, chilled
1 teaspoon chopped garlic
1 cup julienned zucchini
1 cup julienned yellow squash
1 cup julienned red onion
1 teaspoon crushed red pepper
2 pints oysters
chicken stock (page 197) (optional)
16 ounces linguine, cooked al dente
kosher salt to taste
vegetable oil for frying
1 cup masa harina
3 cups all-purpose flour
1/2 cup cornstarch
1/4 cup Creole seasoning
4 ounces bacon, crisp-fried,
    chopped
1/2 cup freshly grated Romano
    cheese

GARNISH

flat-leaf parsley

■ *Serves 4*

Melt 1 tablespoon of the butter in a large sauté pan and add the garlic. Sauté until the garlic is golden brown. Add the zucchini, yellow squash and red onion. Sauté until the vegetables are tender-crisp. Stir in the crushed red pepper.

Drain the oysters and reserve the oyster liquor. Add enough chicken stock if necessary to measure 1 cup liquid. Add the liquid to the sauté pan, stirring to deglaze. Simmer until the liquid begins to reduce, stirring occasionally. Fold in the linguine.

Add the remaining chilled butter and cook until the mixture thickens, stirring vigorously. Season with kosher salt and keep warm over low heat.

Heat the vegetable oil to 350 degrees. Mix the masa harina, flour, cornstarch and Creole seasoning in a large bowl. Coat the oysters with the mixture, shaking off the excess. Fry one oyster to test the temperature of the oil; oysters fried in oil that is too hot will burn and in oil that is not hot enough will be greasy. Fry the remaining oysters in several batches and drain on paper towels.

Spoon the pasta into large bowls. Top with the bacon, Romano cheese and oysters. Garnish with the parsley.

For a lighter version of this dish, fold the oysters in with the linguine instead of frying them, and cook until the edges of the oysters begin to curl.

SEAFOOD COURT-BOUILLON

INGREDIENTS

1 cup (2 sticks) butter
2 cups all-purpose flour
1/2 cup (1 stick) butter
2 tablespoons chopped garlic
1 cup chopped celery
2 cups chopped onions
2 cups chopped bell peppers
8 cups fish stock (page 199)
1 1/2 teaspoons crushed red pepper
1/4 cup chopped fresh thyme
2 lemons, cut into halves
2 cups chopped tomatoes
1 1/2 pounds redfish, chopped
8 ounces (36- to 40-count) shrimp,
    peeled, deveined
8 ounces jumbo crabmeat or
    crab fingers
1 pint oysters
1 cup chopped green onions
1 teaspoon saffron
kosher salt to taste
cooked Louisiana long grain rice

GARNISH

1/2 cup chopped parsley

■ *Serves 10*

Seafood Court-Bouillon also makes a wonderful sauce for grilled or sautéed fish. Just reduce the amount of fish in the court-bouillon. It's also great served over popcorn rice, pasta, roasted potatoes, or even sour cream mashed new potatoes.

Melt 1 cup butter in a saucepot over medium heat and whisk in the flour gradually. Cook for 10 to 15 minutes or until the roux is golden brown, or blond, whisking constantly; remove from the heat.

Melt 1/2 cup butter in a large saucepot and add the garlic, celery, onions and bell peppers. Sauté until the vegetables are tender. Stir in the fish stock, crushed red pepper and thyme and bring to a boil. Whisk a small amount of the hot mixture into the roux; stir the roux into the hot mixture.

Add the lemons and reduce the heat to a simmer. Add the tomatoes, redfish and shrimp. Simmer over low heat until the fish flakes easily, stirring frequently. Stir in the crabmeat, oysters, green onions, and saffron. Simmer for 10 minutes or until the edges of the oysters begin to curl.

Season with kosher salt and discard the lemons. Serve over Louisiana long grain rice and garnish with parsley.

AS THE TEMPERATURE RISES OUTSIDE, SO DOES THE HEAT IN THE

KITCHEN. DINERS LOOKING IN THROUGH THE LARGE WINDOW TO THE

KITCHEN OBSERVE A CERTAIN THEATRE. CHEFS, COOKS, MANAGERS

AND WAITSTAFF MOVE ABOUT, EXECUTING THEIR ASSIGNED TASKS.

THE SOUNDS OF A FILLED DINING ROOM MEET THOSE OF THE

KITCHEN AS THE WAITSTAFF MOVES FROM THE KITCHEN TO THE

DINING ROOM WITH FILLED TRAYS.

ENTRÉES

REVEILLON: A CREOLE CHRISTMAS MENU

New Orleans, Louisiana

The Reveillon is a much-celebrated dining tradition in New Orleans, dating back to the mid-1800s. The traditional Creole meal was originally celebrated twice during the holiday season, once on Christmas Eve and again on New Year's Eve. Today, we celebrate the Reveillon throughout the month of December with a more contemporary version of the traditional New Orleans holiday menu offered at dinner.

MENU

*Beef Daube Glace with Arugula, Pickled Vegetables
and Cracked Black Pepper Crackers*

Smoked Mirliton Soup with Bacon and Bayou Oysters

Fresh Cranberry Salad

*Pan-Seared Duck Breast served with
Herb Spaetzle, Brussels Sprouts and Wild Mushrooms,
topped with Duck Confit and a Fig Reduction*

*Double-Cut Pork Chop served on
Black-Eyed Pea Ragoût and garnished with Vegetable Crisps*

*Pan-Roasted Gulf Fish served on
Wild Rice, Spinach, Sweet Potatoes, Turnips and Shallots in a Caramelized Onion Broth*

Apple-Calvados Tart with Maple Ice Cream and Cranberry Confit

TRIBUTE TO
TENNESSEE WILLIAMS

New Orleans, Louisiana

Every spring, New Orleanians celebrate and pay tribute to one of New Orleans famous literary sons, Tennessee Williams. The New Orleans Tennessee Williams Literary Festival gathers writers, agents, editors and other professionals together with classes and performances during the several days of the festival. We create a menu in honor of this celebration, which takes place not far from Palace Café.

MENU

Oysters in a Glass Menagerie (Oyster Shooters)

Hoppin' John Salad

Étouffée Vieux Carré

Chicken Bonne Femme

Catfish on a Hot Tin Roof

Lady Baltimore Cake

ALLIGATOR GRILLADES WITH JALAPEÑO CORN GRITS

JALAPEÑO CORN GRITS

1 teaspoon butter
1 teaspoon minced jalalpeño pepper
1/2 cup fresh corn kernels
1/4 cup finely chopped onion
1/2 cup uncooked white or
    yellow grits
1 1/2 cups water
1 teaspoon fresh thyme
kosher salt to taste

ALLIGATOR GRILLADES

2 medium tomatoes
vegetable oil
1 1/4 pounds alligator tail meat,
    thinly sliced
1 cup all-purpose flour
6 tablespoons Creole seasoning
1/4 cup (about) vegetable oil
1 cup white wine
1 tablespoon chopped garlic
1 cup mixed julienned red, green
    and yellow bell peppers
1 cup julienned red onion
1 cup chicken stock (page 197) or
    canned chicken broth
1 cup chopped green onions
1 tablespoon fresh thyme
1 tablespoon chopped fresh parsley
kosher salt and cracked black
    pepper to taste
2 tablespoons butter, chopped,
    chilled

■ *Serves 4*

FOR THE GRITS, melt the butter in a medium saucepot. Add the jalapeño pepper, corn and onion. Sauté until the vegetables are tender. Stir in the grits. Add the water gradually, stirring constantly. Cook over medium heat until the grits have absorbed all the water, stirring constantly. Stir in the thyme and season with kosher salt.

FOR THE GRILLADES, core the tomatoes, cut into halves and rub with a small amount of vegetable oil. Make a small slit in the skin of each and arrange cut side down in a baking pan. Roast at 400 degrees until the skins blister. Cool, remove the skins, squeeze out the seeds and chop.

Place the alligator meat between 2 sheets of plastic wrap and pound with a meat mallet to tenderize. Mix the flour with 2 tablespoons of the Creole seasoning and season the alligator meat with the remaining 4 tablespoons Creole seasoning. Coat the alligator meat with the seasoned flour, shaking off the excess.

Heat 1/4 cup vegetable oil, or just enough to cover the bottom of your pot, in a large saucepot and add the alligator meat. Sauté until light brown on both sides. Add the wine, stirring to deglaze the saucepot. Add the garlic, bell peppers, onion and roasted tomatoes. Cook for 5 to 7 minutes.

Stir in the chicken stock and cook until the sauce begins to thicken. Add the green onions, thyme and parsley. Season with kosher salt and cracked pepper. Stir in the butter to richen the sauce. Serve with or on the Jalapeño Corn Grits.

We serve Pork Grillades with Andouille Goat Cheese Grits (page 41) at our Jazz Brunch and run Alligator Grillades with Jalapeño Corn Grits as a dinner special in the fall, when alligator is in season.

GARLIC-CRUSTED FROG LEGS

INGREDIENTS

6 frog saddles (12 frog legs)
1 cup buttermilk
2 medium tomatoes
vegetable oil
2 artichoke bottoms, sliced
2 tablespoons roasted garlic
1 tablespoon butter
1/4 cup chopped fresh basil
kosher salt and cracked black
    pepper to taste
2 cups all-purpose flour
1/2 cup chopped garlic
1 tablespoon kosher salt
2 tablespoons cracked black pepper
1/2 cup vegetable oil
1/4 cup Basil Oil (page 194)

■ *Serves 2*

Cut the saddles from the frog legs with kitchen shears or a sharp knife. Rinse the legs with cold water and combine with the buttermilk in a bowl. Marinate, covered, in the refrigerator for 2 hours.

Core the tomatoes, cut into halves and rub the skins with a small amount of vegetable oil. Make a slit in the skin of each and arrange cut side down in a baking pan. Roast at 400 degrees until the skins blister. Cool, remove the skins, squeeze out the seeds and tear into small pieces.

Sauté the roasted tomatoes, artichoke bottoms and roasted garlic in the butter in a small nonstick sauté pan. Stir in the fresh basil and season with kosher salt and cracked pepper to taste.

Mix the flour, chopped garlic, 1 tablespoon kosher salt and 2 tablespoons cracked pepper in a mixing bowl. Drain the frog legs and coat with the flour mixture, shaking off the excess. Heat 1/2 cup vegetable oil in a sauté pan over high heat. Add the frog legs and sauté until golden brown on all sides; drain on paper towels.

To serve, mound the sautéed vegetables on serving plates. Arrange the frog legs upright against the vegetables and drizzle with the Basil Oil.

GRILLED FILET MIGNON WITH ROASTED SHIITAKE MUSHROOMS

MASHED SOUR CREAM NEW POTATOES

1 1/2 pounds new potatoes
1 cup sour cream
2 tablespoons butter
1/2 cup sliced green onions
kosher salt and cracked black
    pepper to taste

ROASTED SHIITAKE MUSHROOMS

2 cups sliced shiitake mushrooms
2 tablespoons vegetable oil
kosher salt and cracked black
    pepper to taste
1/4 cup julienned shallots
2 tablespoons vegetable oil

GRILLED FILET MIGNON

4 (8-ounce) center-cut filet mignon
kosher salt and cracked black
    pepper to taste
1/2 cup crumbled bleu cheese
1 cup red wine demi-glace
    (page 200)

GARNISH

4 sprigs of fresh thyme

■ *Serves 4*

FOR THE POTATOES, combine the new potatoes with water to cover in a large saucepot and cook until the potatoes are fork-tender. Drain and remove to a mixing bowl. Mash the potatoes with a wooden spoon. Add the sour cream, butter and green onions and mix well. Season with kosher salt and cracked pepper.

FOR THE MUSHROOMS, preheat the oven to 350 degrees. Toss the mushrooms with the 2 tablespoons vegetable oil and kosher salt and cracked pepper to taste in a bowl. Spread evenly on a baking sheet and roast for 10 to 15 minutes or until the mushrooms begin to dry. Cool to room temperature. Sauté the shallots in 2 tablespoons vegetable oil in a sauté pan over medium heat for 5 to 10 minutes or until tender. Stir in the roasted mushrooms.

FOR THE FILET MIGNON, season the steaks on both sides with kosher salt and cracked pepper. Grill or broil until done to taste.

To serve, spoon the potatoes into the centers of 4 serving plates. Place 1 steak on the potatoes on each plate, top with the mushrooms and crumble the bleu cheese over the steaks. Ladle the demi-glace over the steaks and garnish with the thyme.

In the restaurant, we have the luxury of always having several demi-glaces on hand to enhance dishes such as this one. The recipe for the red wine demi-glace is on page 200, but if you don't have time to make it or can't find it in a specialty or gourmet store, you can finish the dish with an herb or garlic butter or with the natural juices from the meat and roasted mushrooms.

GRILLED RIB-EYE WITH ROASTED NEW POTATO PORT SALUT HASH

HOMEMADE STEAK SAUCE

1/4 cup (1/2 stick) butter
3 Vidalia onions, chopped
1 jalapeño pepper, chopped
1/2 cup roasted garlic
6 medium-large tomatoes, chopped
1 1/2 cups tomato paste
1 cup cane vinegar
1 cup Worcestershire sauce
1 1/2 cups molasses
1 gallon veal stock (page 199)
2 ounces each fresh tarragon, basil
    and oregano, chopped
kosher salt and black pepper to taste

NEW POTATO HASH

1 1/2 pounds new potatoes
2 tablespoons vegetable oil
kosher salt and cracked black
    pepper to taste
4 ounces bacon
1 large onion, julienned
6 ounces Port Salut cheese, chopped
1/2 cup chopped fresh parsley

GRILLED RIB-EYES

4 (12-ounce) Black Angus rib-eye
    steaks
kosher salt and cracked black
    pepper to taste

■ *Serves 4*

FOR THE SAUCE, melt the butter in a large saucepot and add the onions, jalapeño pepper and roasted garlic. Sauté until the vegetables are tender. Add the tomatoes and bring to a boil. Reduce the heat and simmer for 10 minutes. Stir in the tomato paste and simmer for 5 to 10 minutes.

Add the cane vinegar, Worcestershire sauce, molasses, veal stock, tarragon, basil and oregano; mix well. Cook, covered, over medium heat for 30 minutes. Cook, uncovered, for 30 minutes longer.

Purée the sauce and return to the saucepot. Cook over medium-high heat until reduced by 1/2. Strain through a fine strainer into a saucepot. Cook until the sauce thickens to the desired consistency. Season with kosher salt and cracked pepper. Store in the refrigerator.

FOR THE HASH, cut the new potatoes into quarters. Toss with the vegetable oil, kosher salt and cracked pepper in a bowl. Spread the potatoes on a baking sheet. Roast at 400 degrees for 20 to 30 minutes or until tender and golden brown. Cook the bacon in a large sauté pan until crisp; remove and chop the bacon, reserving the drippings in the sauté pan. Add the onion to the drippings in the sauté pan and cook until caramelized. Add the roasted potatoes, bacon, Port Salut cheese and parsley. Cook, covered, for 5 to 10 minutes or until the cheese melts. Mix gently and season with kosher salt and cracked pepper. Keep warm.

FOR THE RIB-EYES, preheat the grill. Season the steaks on all sides with kosher salt and cracked pepper. Grill the steaks until done to taste. Serve the steaks with the new potato hash and the Homemade Steak Sauce.

BEEF WELLINGTON

MUSHROOM DUXELLES

2 tablespoons blend of 80%
    vegetable oil and 20% olive oil,
    or butter
2 tablespoons minced shallots
16 ounces mixed or domestic
    mushrooms, minced
1 1/2 cups marsala
1 teaspoon minced fresh rosemary
kosher salt and cracked black
    pepper to taste

BEEF WELLINGTON

4 (6-ounce) center-cut filets of beef
    tenderloin
kosher salt and cracked black
    pepper to taste
4 (6x6-inch) squares puff pastry
1 egg, lightly beaten
2 tablespoons butter
8 each baby carrots, sunburst squash
    and baby zucchini
8 shallots, caramelized
1 cup red wine demi-glace
    (page 200)
4 ounces bleu cheese, crumbled
4 sprigs of flat-leaf parsley

■ *Serves 4*

FOR THE MUSHROOMS, heat the oil blend in a sauté pan and add the shallots. Sauté until the shallots are tender. Add the mushrooms and cook, covered, for 5 to 7 minutes or until tender. Add the wine, stirring to deglaze the skillet. Cook until most of the liquid has evaporated. Stir in the rosemary and season with kosher salt and cracked pepper.

FOR THE BEEF, season the steaks on all sides with kosher salt and cracked pepper. Grill or sear the steaks just until the juices are sealed in; the centers should be quite rare.

Spoon 1/2 cup of the Mushroom Duxelles into the centers of the puff pastry squares and place a steak in the center of each. Fold the puff pastry to enclose the steak and mushroom duxelles.

Brush with the egg and place in a baking pan. Bake at 350 degrees for 15 to 20 minutes for medium-rare to medium.

Melt the butter in a sauté pan and add the carrots, squash, zucchini and shallots. Sauté until the vegetables are tender. Season with kosher salt and cracked pepper.

Place 1 beef pastry on each of 4 serving plates. Arrange the vegetables around the beef. Drizzle with the demi-glace and sprinkle with the bleu cheese. Top with the parsley.

Beef Wellington was served at one of Dickie and Leslie Brennan's Christmas dinner parties. Although Chef Gus made a personal appearance to prepare it, we think you'll definitely be able to cook this dish on your own. The only tricky part is cooking the beef to your preferred temperature. Some puff pastry takes longer to bake and can result in overcooked beef. Remember to sear the beef just long enough to seal in the juices. It should still be quite rare when you wrap it in the pastry and will finish cooking in the oven.

140

Tournedos of Beef with Horseradish Mashed Potatoes

Horseradish Mashed Potatoes

1 1/2 pounds Idaho potatoes, peeled
1/2 cup (1 stick) butter
1/2 cup warm milk
3 tablespoons prepared horseradish
kosher salt and white pepper to taste

Garlic Aïoli Croutons

2 egg yolks
juice of 1 lemon
1 teaspoon vinegar
1/2 teaspoon dry mustard
1 cup vegetable oil
1/4 cup roasted garlic, puréed
kosher salt and white pepper to taste
8 (1-inch) rounds French bread

Steamed Asparagus

1 tablespoon butter
1/4 cup water
12 jumbo spears fresh asparagus
kosher salt and cracked black
    pepper to taste

FOR THE POTATOES, combine the potatoes with water to cover in a saucepot and cook until fork-tender; drain. Mash the potatoes in a large bowl. Add the butter, warm milk and horseradish and mix well with a wooden spoon. Season with kosher salt and white pepper. Keep warm until serving time.

FOR THE CROUTONS, whisk the egg yolks, lemon juice, vinegar and dry mustard in a bowl. Whisk in half the vegetable oil gradually. Stir in the roasted garlic. Whisk in the remaining vegetable oil gradually; the aïoli will break if the oil is added too quickly. Season with kosher salt and white pepper.

Brush the tops of the bread rounds with the aïoli and arrange on a baking sheet. Bake at 350 degrees for 20 to 25 minutes or until crisp and dry.

FOR THE ASPARAGUS, melt the butter in the water in a sauté pan over medium-high heat. Add the asparagus and season with kosher salt and cracked pepper. Reduce the heat and steam for 5 minutes or until tender.

TOURNEDOS OF BEEF

1 medium red onion, sliced
1 medium Vidalia onion, sliced
1/4 cup vegetable oil
8 (3-ounce) tournedos of beef
kosher salt and cracked black
    pepper to taste
2 cups Choron Sauce (page 193)

GARNISH

4 sprigs of flat-leaf parsley

■ *Serves 4*

FOR THE BEEF, grill the red onion and Vidalia onion lightly and reserve. Add the vegetable oil to a cast-iron skillet and heat over medium-high heat. Season the tournedos on all sides with kosher salt and cracked pepper. Add to the skillet and sear on both sides. Cook until nearly done to taste then add the onions to the skillet. Cook until the onions are caramelized.

To serve, spoon the Horseradish Mashed Potatoes onto 4 serving plates. Place 2 Garlic Aïoli Croutons next to the potatoes on each plate and top the croutons with the tournedos. Spoon the Choron Sauce over the tournedos and top with the grilled onions. Arrange 3 spears of Steamed Asparagus between the potatoes and the tournedos. Garnish with the parsley.

For a lighter version of this dish, substitute seared tomatoes for the Garlic Aïoli Croutons and skip the Choron Sauce. If you're not a tomato person, go with a béarnaise or hollandaise sauce instead of the choron. Try different combinations of potato side dishes and vegetables. Change up the flavors. Cook what tastes good to you!

GRILLED PORK CHOPS WITH SAUTÉED CABBAGE

APPLE DEMI-GLACE

2 cups finely chopped onions
1 cup finely chopped celery
1 cup finely chopped carrots
2 bay leaves
1 tablespoon whole black
    peppercorns
2 cups red wine
4 gallons veal stock (page 199)
2 sprigs of fresh thyme
6 cups sliced apples

GRILLED PORK CHOPS

1 tablespoon butter
4 cups julienned Napa cabbage
1 cup julienned red onion
2 tablespoons chicken stock
    (page 197) or canned
    chicken broth
2 tablespoons rice wine vinegar
1/2 cup chopped crisp-fried bacon
kosher salt and cracked black
    pepper to taste
8 center-cut cold smoked pork chops

■ *Serves 4*

FOR THE DEMI-GLACE, combine the chopped onions, celery and carrots in a nonstick 5-gallon stockpot and cook, covered, over high heat until caramelized. Add the bay leaves and peppercorns. Add the red wine and stir to deglaze the stockpot. Cook until the liquid is reduced by 1/2.

Add the veal stock and simmer for 2 1/2 to 3 hours or until the liquid is reduced to 2 quarts with the consistency of molasses, skimming the surface and adding the thyme sprigs during the last 30 minutes of cooking time. Strain through a fine strainer into a saucepot. Add the apples and simmer over low heat for an additional 20 to 30 minutes. Store unused portions in the refrigerator.

FOR THE PORK CHOPS, melt the butter in a large sauté pan and add the cabbage and red onion. Sauté until the vegetables are tender. Add the chicken stock and rice wine vinegar and stir to deglaze the sauté pan. Add the bacon and season with kosher salt and cracked pepper. Keep warm over low heat.

Season the pork chops on both sides with kosher salt and cracked pepper. Grill until cooked through.

Spoon the cabbage onto serving plates and cross 2 pork chops over the cabbage. Drizzle with the Apple Demi-Glace.

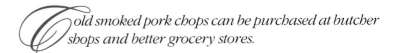

Cold smoked pork chops can be purchased at butcher shops and better grocery stores.

DOUBLE-CUT PORK CHOPS WITH BLACK-EYED PEA RAGOÛT

BLACK-EYED PEA RAGOÛT

8 ounces fresh black-eyed peas
4 ounces chopped bacon
1 tablespoon chopped garlic
1 cup mixed chopped red, green
    and yellow bell peppers
1 cup sliced leeks
1 cup chicken stock (page 197) or
    canned chicken broth
1 cup (2 sticks) butter, chilled,
    chopped
1 cup sliced green onions
1/2 cup mixed chopped fresh basil,
    oregano and thyme
kosher salt and cracked black
    pepper to taste

GREEN ONION POPCORN RICE

1/2 cup (1 stick) butter
2 cups uncooked popcorn rice
3 cups water
1 cup sliced green onions

DOUBLE-CUT PORK CHOPS

1 (6 1/2-pound) pork loin
1 cup chopped garlic
1/2 cup minced rosemary
kosher salt and cracked black
    pepper to taste

■ *Serves 6*

FOR THE RAGOÛT, blanch the black-eyed peas in water to cover in a saucepot; drain. Cook the bacon in a large sauté pan until crisp. Remove the bacon. Strain the drippings; reserve 2 tablespoons drippings and the bacon. Add the reserved drippings to a large sauté pan and stir in the garlic. Sauté until light brown. Add the bell peppers, leeks and black-eyed peas. Sauté for 10 minutes.

Add the chicken stock, stirring to deglaze the skillet. Cook until the liquid has nearly evaporated. Stir in the butter and reserved bacon. Stir in the green onions and chopped fresh herbs. Season with kosher salt and cracked pepper. Keep warm.

FOR THE RICE, melt the butter in a medium saucepot. Add the rice and sauté for 2 minutes. Add the water and cook, uncovered, over medium-high heat until the water is absorbed and the rice is tender. Let stand, covered, until serving time. Stir in the green onions just before serving.

FOR THE PORK CHOPS, preheat the oven to 350 degrees. Rub the pork loin on all sides with the garlic, rosemary, kosher salt and cracked pepper. Place in a baking pan and insert a meat thermometer into the thickest portion. Roast for 40 to 45 minutes or to 150 degrees on the meat thermometer. Let rest for 10 minutes before slicing.

To serve, slice the pork loin into double-cut chops. Serve with the Black-Eyed Pea Ragoût and Green Onion Popcorn Rice.

You can also use dried black-eyed peas in this recipe when fresh peas aren't available. Just soak the peas and cook them in water to cover until tender.

145

PALACE POTATO PIE

POTATO PIE

1 (5- to 7-pound) Boston pork butt
kosher salt and cracked black
    pepper or Creole seasoning
    to taste
8 cups chicken stock (page 197) or
    canned chicken broth
1 cup roasted garlic
3 pounds Idaho potatoes, peeled
1 cup (2 sticks) butter
1 cup warm milk
3 cups fresh spinach
2 cups shredded Cheddar cheese

ONION GRAVY

1/2 cup (1 stick) butter
1/2 cup all-purpose flour
4 cups julienned yellow onions
2 tablespoons blend of 80%
    vegetable oil and 20% olive oil
1 3/4 cups chicken stock (page 197)
    or canned chicken broth
1 cup veal stock (page 199) or
    canned beef broth
sugar to taste
kosher salt and cracked black
    pepper to taste

■ *Serves 8 to 10*

FOR THE PIE, season the pork butt on all sides with kosher salt and cracked pepper or Creole seasoning. Place in a large baking dish and bake, uncovered, at 350 degrees for 45 to 55 minutes. Add enough chicken stock to fill the baking dish halfway. Bake, covered with foil, for 1 hour. Add the roasted garlic and bake, uncovered, for 30 minutes longer or until the meat is very tender and falling easily from the bone. Cool to room temperature and remove the meat from the bone.

Cook the potatoes in water to cover in a saucepot until fork-tender; drain. Mash in a large mixing bowl until smooth. Add the butter and warm milk and mix well. Season with kosher salt and cracked pepper. Wilt the spinach lightly in a nonstick sauté pan over low heat.

Layer the pork, potatoes and spinach in a baking dish. Top with the cheese. Broil until the cheese melts.

FOR THE GRAVY, melt the butter in a small saucepot and whisk in the flour gradually. Cook over medium heat for 3 minutes or until pale golden brown, or blond, with a toasty smell. Remove roux from the heat.

Sauté the onions in the oil blend in a large saucepot until caramelized. Add the chicken stock and veal stock and mix well. Simmer over medium heat for 5 to 10 minutes.

Whisk a small amount of the hot mixture into the roux, then whisk the roux into the hot mixture. Cook until thickened, stirring constantly. Season with sugar, kosher salt and cracked pepper. Reduce the heat and keep warm. Serve the gravy on the side or ladle around each serving of the pie.

Palace Potato Pie is Southern comfort food at its finest. We have had it on our lunch menu for years, and we know better than to take it off! It can be served in individual baking dishes or family-style in a casserole dish as we've done here.

PANÉED RABBIT WITH BRANDY CREAM FETTUCCINE

BRANDY CREAM

1 tablespoon butter
1/4 cup chopped onion
1/4 cup chopped carrot
1/4 cup chopped celery
1/4 cup mushroom stems
1 sprig of fresh thyme
1/2 teaspoon minced garlic
1/4 cup brandy
1/2 cup veal demi-glace
   (page 200), or store-bought
   demi-glace
1 1/4 cups heavy cream
1/2 teaspoon kosher salt
1/4 teaspoon white pepper

FETTUCCINE

1/4 cup finely chopped carrot
1/2 cup sliced mushrooms
1 teaspoon vegetable oil
kosher salt and cracked black
   pepper to taste
1/4 cup sliced leeks
1/4 cup fresh English peas or frozen
   green peas
1 tablespoon butter
4 ounces fettuccine, cooked al dente
1 tablespoon Creole mustard

FOR THE BRANDY CREAM, melt the butter in a small saucepot. Add the onion, carrot, celery, mushroom stems, thyme and garlic and sauté until the vegetables are tender. Add the brandy and ignite; allow the flames to subside.

Add the veal demi-glace and heavy cream and mix well. Bring to a boil and reduce the heat. Simmer for 20 minutes or until thickened enough to coat the spoon. Pour through a fine strainer, pressing the sautéed vegetables to release their juices. Season with the kosher salt and white pepper.

FOR THE FETTUCCINE, cook the carrot in water in a saucepot for 10 minutes or until tender-crisp; drain. Toss the mushrooms with the vegetable oil and a small amount of kosher salt and cracked pepper. Spread evenly in a baking pan and roast at 350 degrees for 10 minutes or until the mushrooms begin to dry.

Sauté the carrot, leeks, mushrooms and peas in the butter in a large sauté pan until tender. Stir in 1/2 cup of the Brandy Cream and fettuccine. Cook for 5 minutes or until heated through. Adjust the seasoning and fold in the Creole mustard.

Panéed Rabbit

1 (3- to 4-pound) rabbit
1 tablespoon (or more) Creole
    seasoning
4 ounces tasso, sliced
2 ounces Gruyère cheese, cut into
    2 (1-ounce) slices
1/2 cup all-purpose flour
1 teaspoon Creole seasoning
2 eggs
1 cup milk
1 cup bread crumbs
1 teaspoon Creole seasoning
1/4 cup vegetable oil

Garnish

2 tablespoons freshly grated Romano
    cheese
2 tablespoons finely chopped red
    bell pepper
2 tablespoons chopped fresh parsley

■ *Serves 2*

For the rabbit, debone the rabbit, removing the tenderloins and legs for a total of 4 pieces. Place between 2 pieces of plastic wrap and pound lightly with a meat mallet. Season on both sides with 1 tablespoon or more Creole seasoning. Layer the tasso and Gruyère cheese on the leg pieces and top each with a tenderloin piece.

Season the flour with 1 teaspoon Creole seasoning in a bowl. Whisk the eggs with the milk in a bowl. Mix the bread crumbs with 1 teaspoon Creole seasoning in a bowl. Coat the layered rabbit pieces with the seasoned flour, shaking off the excess, dip into the egg wash and press the bread crumbs onto the surface to coat well. Chill, covered, in the refrigerator.

Heat the vegetable oil in a large ovenproof sauté pan over medium-high heat. Add the breaded rabbit and sauté until golden brown on both sides. Finish by roasting in a 350-degree oven for 10 to 20 minutes or until cooked through. Keep warm.

To serve, spoon the Brandy Cream Fettuccine onto the serving plates and place the rabbit on the pasta. Garnish with the Romano cheese, bell pepper and parsley.

Over the years, we've cooked rabbit all kinds of different ways but have found that panéed rabbit is by far the most moist and juicy. To change the flavor of the dish, use smoked Gouda cheese or mozzarella instead of Romano. If you don't like rabbit or have a hard time finding it, substitute chicken to prepare the dish.

GRILLED VEAL CHOPS WITH ROCK SHRIMP RISOTTO

ROCK SHRIMP RISOTTO

5 cups chicken stock (page 197),
    crab stock (page 196) or
    canned chicken broth
1/2 cup finely chopped onion
2 tablespoons butter
2 cups uncooked arborio rice
8 ounces rock shrimp, peeled,
    deveined
1/2 cup white wine
kosher salt and white pepper to taste

SAUTÉED VEGETABLES

1 large red bell pepper
2 cups oyster mushrooms
1 cup chopped green onion tops
1 tablespoon butter
kosher salt and cracked black
    pepper to taste

VEAL CHOPS

4 (12-ounce) center-cut veal chops
kosher salt and cracked black
    pepper to taste
1 cup red wine demi-glace
    (page 200)

■ *Serves 4*

We serve our veal chops medium unless requested to do otherwise. This dish can be finished with an herb butter, garlic butter, lemon butter or the natural juices in the dish if you don't have the red wine demi-glace.

FOR THE RISOTTO, bring the chicken or crab stock to a boil in a saucepot and reduce the heat; maintain the temperature at a low simmer. Sauté the onion in the butter in a medium saucepot until tender. Add the rice and sauté over low heat for 5 minutes, stirring constantly with a wooden spoon.

Increase the heat to medium-high and add the hot stock to the rice 1 or 2 cups at a time, cooking until all the stock is absorbed after each addition. Stir constantly and add the rock shrimp and wine when the rice begins to become tender; the entire process will require about 30 minutes. Cook until the shrimp are cooked through. Season with kosher salt and white pepper. Cover and keep warm.

FOR THE VEGETABLES, cut the bell pepper into halves, discarding the stem, membranes and seeds. Place cut side down on a baking sheet and roast at 400 degrees until the skin blisters. Cool, remove the skin and julienne the bell pepper. Sauté the roasted bell pepper, mushrooms and green onion tops in the butter in a sauté pan. Season with kosher salt and cracked black pepper.

FOR THE VEAL CHOPS, season the chops on both sides with kosher salt and cracked pepper. Grill over medium-hot coals until medium or until done to taste.

To serve, place the chops on serving plates and ladle the red wine demi-glace over the chops. Top with the sautéed vegetables and serve with the Rock Shrimp Risotto.

VEAL SCALOPPINE WITH JUMBO LUMP CRABMEAT

BÉARNAISE SAUCE

2 cups (4 sticks) butter
1 cup chopped tarragon
1 tablespoon chopped shallots
1 cup red wine vinegar
1 teaspoon cracked black pepper
5 egg yolks
1/4 cup water
1/2 teaspoon salt
kosher salt and cracked black
    pepper to taste

VEAL SCALOPPINE

1/2 cup (about) vegetable oil
1 cup all-purpose flour
1 tablespoon Creole seasoning
8 (3- to 4-ounce) veal scallops
kosher salt and cracked black
    pepper to taste
2 tablespoons butter
2 cups mixed sliced wild mushrooms
1/4 cup white wine
8 ounces jumbo lump crabmeat
1 teaspoon fresh thyme

GARNISH

1/2 cup chopped green onions

■ *Serves 4*

FOR THE SAUCE, melt the butter in a large sauté pan over low heat. Skim the foam from the surface and discard. Pour the clear butter from the solids, which will sink to the bottom of the pan. Cool slightly.

Combine the tarragon, shallots, red wine vinegar and 1 teaspoon cracked pepper in a saucepot over medium heat and cook until the mixture has reduced and the vinegar has cooked off, stirring frequently. Cool to room temperature.

Whisk the egg yolks, water and salt in a double boiler or metal bowl placed over boiling water. Cook until the egg yolks almost triple in volume and turn pale yellow, whisking constantly; remove from the heat if necessary during the cooking process to reduce the temperature and prevent the eggs from scrambling.

Remove from the heat and whisk in the clarified butter gradually; the sauce should have a thick and creamy consistency. Stir in the tarragon reduction. Season with salt and cracked pepper to taste. Keep warm.

FOR THE VEAL, heat 1/2 cup vegetable oil, or enough to cover the bottom, in a large skillet. Mix the flour with the Creole seasoning in a shallow dish. Season the veal scallops on both sides with kosher salt and cracked pepper and coat with the seasoned flour, shaking off the excess. Sauté in the oil in the skillet until golden brown on both sides.

Melt the butter in a medium sauté pan. Add the mushrooms and sauté until tender. Add the white wine, stirring to deglaze the skillet. Fold in the crabmeat and fresh thyme. Cover and steam for 5 minutes.

To serve, place the veal scallops on serving plates and top with the crabmeat and mushrooms. Drizzle with the Béarnaise Sauce and garnish with the green onions.

We like to serve our Veal Scaloppine with simple accompaniments, such as steamed asparagus (page 143) and mashed potatoes.

CHICKEN AND ANDOUILLE
ÉTOUFFÉE

INGREDIENTS

1/2 cup vegetable oil
1/2 cup all-purpose flour
1 tablespoon butter
1 cup chopped onion
1 cup chopped celery
1 cup mixed chopped red, green
    and yellow bell peppers
1 tablespoon chopped garlic
3 bay leaves
16 ounces andouille sausage, sliced
1/2 cup tomato paste
1 teaspoon crushed red pepper
8 cups chicken stock (page 197) or
    canned chicken broth
1 tablespoon fresh thyme
16 ounces boneless skinless chicken
    breasts, cut into bite-size pieces
kosher salt to taste

■ *Serves 4*

Heat the vegetable oil in a small saucepot over medium heat. Whisk in the flour gradually. Cook until the roux is dark amber in color, whisking constantly; remove from the heat.

Melt the butter in a large saucepot. Add the onion, celery, bell peppers, garlic, bay leaves and andouille and sauté until the vegetables are tender and the sausage is brown.

Stir the roux into the vegetables and sausage. Add the tomato paste and crushed red pepper and mix well. Cook for 5 minutes, stirring occasionally. Stir in the chicken stock, fresh thyme and chicken.

Bring to a boil and reduce the heat. Simmer until the chicken is cooked through, skimming the surface and stirring occasionally. Season with kosher salt to taste and discard the bay leaves. Serve over rice, pasta or jambalaya.

Chef Gus prepared Chicken and Andouille Étouffée at Jazz Fest 1999. This is a great base recipe for étouffée. For crawfish étouffée, substitute two pounds of crawfish tails for the chicken and andouille. For shrimp étouffée, substitute two pounds of peeled large shrimp for the chicken and andouille, and substitute seafood stock for the chicken stock.

CHICKEN BONNE FEMME

INGREDIENTS

1 cup all-purpose flour
1 tablespoon Creole seasoning
2 (7-ounce) chicken breast fillets, trimmed
kosher salt and cracked black pepper to taste
1/4 cup olive oil
1/4 cup roasted garlic cloves
1 cup wild mushrooms
1/2 cup mixed julienned red, green and yellow bell peppers
1 cup new potatoes, cut into quarters, roasted
1/2 cup leeks, cut into half-moon slices
1/2 cup white portions of green onions, cut into 3-inch pieces
1 cup chicken stock (page 197) or canned chicken broth
2 teaspoons chopped fresh herbs, such as tarragon, chervil, chives and/or parsley

■ *Serves 2*

Preheat the oven to 350 degrees. Mix the flour with the Creole seasoning in a shallow dish. Season the chicken with kosher salt and cracked pepper and coat with the flour mixture, shaking off the excess.

Heat a 9-inch ovenproof French sauté pan and add the olive oil. Add the chicken to the pan and sear for 2 minutes or until golden brown on the bottom. Add the garlic, mushrooms, bell peppers, new potatoes, leeks and green onions on and around the chicken.

Remove the chicken from the sauté pan and place seared side up on top of the vegetables. Ladle the chicken stock into the pan and sprinkle with the herbs, kosher salt and cracked pepper.

Roast in the oven for 8 to 10 minutes or until the chicken is cooked through. Serve in the sauté pan or remove to serving plates.

The term "bonne femme" is used to describe simply prepared rustic dishes that are most often served from the pan or dish in which they are cooked. We offer this dish at lunch during the New Orleans Tennessee Williams Literary Festival since Tennessee makes reference to Chicken Bonne Femme in his play Vieux Carré.

153

MARINATED POUSSIN WITH NEW ORLEANS OYSTER DRESSING

OYSTER DRESSING

2 1/2 loaves French bread, sliced
1/2 cup (1 stick) butter
1 tablespoon chopped garlic
1 cup chopped celery
1 cup chopped onion
1 1/2 pints oysters
chicken stock (page 197) or canned
    chicken broth
6 bay leaves
1 tablespoon thyme
2 cups chopped green onions
kosher salt and cracked black
    pepper to taste

MARINATED POUSSIN

1/4 cup vegetable oil
1/2 cup equal parts mixed chopped
    thyme, basil and oregano
1 tablespoon chopped garlic
kosher salt and cracked black
    pepper to taste
4 poussin, deboned
2 cups chicken stock (page 197) or
    canned chicken broth
1 tablespoon roasted garlic
1 tablespoon fresh thyme
1 tablespoon chopped chilled butter

GARNISH

4 sprigs of flat-leaf parsley

■ *Serves 4*

FOR THE OYSTER DRESSING, process the French bread into fine crumbs in a food processor. Melt the butter in a medium saucepot and add the garlic. Sauté until the garlic is light brown. Add the celery and onion and sauté until tender.

Drain the oysters, reserving the liquor. Add enough chicken stock to the reserved liquor if necessary to measure 1 cup liquid. Add the oysters, oyster liquor, bay leaves and thyme to the saucepot and mix well. Bring to a boil and reduce the heat. Fold in the bread crumbs and green onions. Season with kosher salt and cracked pepper. Cook until heated through. Discard the bay leaves before serving.

FOR THE POUSSIN, whisk the vegetable oil, mixed herbs, garlic, kosher salt and cracked pepper in a bowl. Add the poussin, turning to coat well. Marinate, covered, in the refrigerator for 1 hour or longer.

Combine the chicken stock and roasted garlic in a large saucepot and cook over medium-high heat until reduced by 1/2. Add the thyme. Whisk in the butter to richen the sauce and cook until the butter is completely incorporated. Season with kosher salt and cracked pepper.

Drain the poussin. Grill until marked, then turn 1/4 turn to mark in a diamond pattern. Turn the poussin over and grill until cooked through and the juices run clear.

Spoon the dressing onto serving plates and place the poussin on top. Ladle the reduced chicken stock over the poussin and garnish with the parsley.

New Orleans Oyster Dressing is also one of our Thanksgiving menu mainstays, as well as one of our favorite dishes to serve with Grilled Filet Mignon (page 138).

SMOKED CHICKEN LASAGNA

LASAGNA

2 cups julienned onions
1/4 cup blend of 80% vegetable oil
    and 20% olive oil
16 ounces lasagna noodles,
    uncooked or cooked al dente
3 pounds smoked chicken, chopped
2 cups julienned roasted red
    bell peppers
2 cups julienned roasted yellow
    bell peppers
2 pounds fresh spinach
3 pounds whole-milk ricotta cheese,
    crumbled
3 cups shredded pepper jack cheese
2 cups shredded mozzarella cheese
1 cup grated Pecorino Romano
    cheese
kosher salt and cracked black
    pepper to taste

MUSHROOM CREAM

1 tablespoon butter
2 teaspoons chopped garlic
2 cups roasted mushrooms
4 cups cream
kosher salt and cracked black
    pepper to taste

GARNISH

flat-leaf parsley

■ *Serves 8 to 10*

FOR THE LASAGNA, sauté the onions in half the oil blend in a sauté pan until caramelized. Coat a 9×11-inch or 9×13-inch baking dish with the remaining oil blend.

Layer the pasta, smoked chicken, roasted bell peppers, caramelized onions, spinach and cheeses 1/4 at a time in the prepared baking dish, sprinkling the layers with kosher salt and cracked pepper to taste. Bake at 300 degrees for 45 to 60 minutes or until bubbly. Remove from the oven and let stand for 20 to 25 minutes or until set.

FOR THE MUSHROOM CREAM, melt the butter in a large saucepot over medium heat. Add the garlic and sauté until light brown. Add the roasted mushrooms. Stir in the cream and cook until the sauce is reduced by 1/2. Season with kosher salt and cracked pepper to taste.

To serve, ladle the mushroom cream onto the serving plates. Cut the lasagna into squares and place on the plates. Garnish with parsley.

To roast the bell peppers for Smoked Chicken Lasagna, cut the peppers into halves, discarding the stems, seeds and membranes. Arrange cut side down on a baking sheet and roast at 400 degrees until the skins blister. Cool, remove the skins and julienne the peppers.

To roast the mushrooms, toss them with salt, pepper and a few tablespoons of vegetable oil and arrange on a baking sheet. Roast at 350 degrees for 10 to 12 minutes or until the mushrooms begin to dry. Cool to room temperature.

Smoke the chicken over wood chips on a grill with the cover down or in a home smoker.

PEPPER-CRUSTED DUCK WITH DUCK CONFIT

DUCK CONFIT

2 bay leaves
1 small bunch fresh thyme
1/2 cup kosher salt
1/2 cup cracked black pepper
legs and thighs of 2 (5- to 7-pound) ducks
2 cups rendered duck fat or blend of 80% vegetable oil and 20% olive oil
2 garlic cloves

PEPPER-CRUSTED DUCK

breasts of 2 (5- to 7-pound) ducks
2 tablespoons coarsely ground black pepper
8 ounces foie gras, sliced into 4 pieces
kosher salt and cracked black pepper to taste
4 cups frisée
1/2 red onion, thinly shaved
sections of 2 oranges
1/2 cup Foie Gras Vinaigrette
1 cup Au Poivre Sauce (page 192)

■ *Serves 4*

FOR THE CONFIT, make a rub by combining the bay leaves, thyme, kosher salt and cracked pepper in a food processor and processing until finely ground. Rub over the duck legs and thighs and let stand, covered, in the refrigerator for 24 hours.

Preheat the oven to 200 to 225 degrees. Place the rendered duck fat and garlic in a baking dish and warm in the oven. Wipe the rub from the duck and add the duck to the baking dish. Roast for 45 to 60 minutes or until the duck is very tender and pulls easily from the bone. Remove the meat from the bone and reserve.

FOR THE DUCK, score the skin of the duck breasts in a crisscross pattern, taking care not to cut the meat. Rub 2 tablespoons coarsely ground pepper onto the skin and into the cuts. Sear the duck skin side down in a large nonstick sauté pan over medium-high heat.

Reduce the heat to medium and cook for 20 minutes or until the fat has been rendered, pouring it off as it renders. Turn the duck over and cook for 3 to 5 minutes longer for rare to medium-rare or until done to taste. Remove to a platter.

Season the foie gras on both sides with kosher salt and cracked pepper. Sear in a nonstick sauté pan over high heat for 45 seconds on each side.

To serve, toss the frisée, red onion, orange sections and Duck Confit with the Foie Gras Vinaigrette in a large bowl. Adjust the seasoning. Spoon the mixture onto serving plates.

Top each plate with a piece of seared foie gras. Slice the duck and fan around the frisée salad. Drizzle with the Au Poivre Sauce.

FOIE GRAS VINAIGRETTE

1/2 ounce foie gras, chopped
2 shallots, chopped
1/3 cup sherry vinegar
2 tablespoons chopped parsley
freshly ground black pepper to taste
2/3 cup olive oil
kosher salt to taste

FOR THE VINAIGRETTE, melt the foie gras in a small saucepan over medium heat. Reduce the heat and add the shallots. Sauté for 2 minutes or until the shallots are translucent. Stir in the vinegar, parsley and pepper. Whisk in the olive oil and season with kosher salt. Cool to room temperature.

MOLASSES-GLAZED DUCK WITH APPLE BACON CABBAGE

DIRTY RICE

3 tablespoons butter
4 ounces pork loin, finely chopped
1 cup finely chopped green bell
    pepper
1 cup finely chopped onion
1/2 cup finely chopped celery
1 teaspoon Creole seasoning
1 tablespoon chopped fresh thyme
3 bay leaves
1 teaspoon cracked black pepper
1 cup uncooked white rice
2 cups chicken stock (page 197) or
    canned chicken broth
1 duck liver, very finely chopped
1 cup thinly sliced green onions
kosher salt to taste

APPLE BACON CABBAGE

6 ounces apple or hickory-smoked
    bacon, finely chopped
2 cups chopped red onion
1 (2-pound) head cabbage, sliced
1/2 cup packed light brown sugar
1/2 cup cane vinegar or apple cider
    vinegar
2 Granny Smith apples, cored,
    sliced
kosher salt and cracked black
    pepper to taste

FOR THE RICE, melt the butter in a large saucepot. Add the pork and sauté lightly. Add the bell pepper, onion and celery and cook until the vegetables are tender. Stir in the Creole seasoning, thyme, bay leaves and cracked pepper. Cook for 5 to 7 minutes. Add the rice and mix well.

Add the chicken stock and bring to a boil. Cook until the liquid is reduced to the level of the top of the rice. Cover and steam for 15 minutes or until the rice is tender. Stir in the duck liver and green onions and cook for 5 minutes. Season with kosher salt and discard the bay leaves.

FOR THE CABBAGE, sauté the bacon in a sauté pan over medium-high heat until crisp. Add the red onion and cook until tender. Add the cabbage, brown sugar and cane vinegar and mix well. Cook until the cabbage is caramelized, stirring frequently. Stir in the apples and season with kosher salt and cracked pepper.

Molasses-Glazed Duck

2 (4- to 5-pound) ducklings
4 bay leaves
1 1/2 cups finely chopped carrots
1 1/2 cups finely chopped onions
1 1/2 cups finely chopped celery
8 garlic cloves
equal parts kosher salt and cracked
    black pepper
1/2 cup soy sauce
1 cup molasses
1/2 cup cane vinegar or apple
    cider vinegar
2 tablespoons vegetable oil

■ *Serves 4*

FOR THE DUCK, remove the neck and giblets from the ducks and rinse well inside and out with cold water. Stuff the duck cavities with the bay leaves, carrots, onions, celery and garlic. Season the outside of the ducks with a rub of equal parts kosher salt and cracked black pepper.

Truss each duck by placing the center of a 2- to 3-foot piece of twine around the remaining portion of the neck. Wrap the twine across the duck in an X, then behind the back and over the wings, pulling it tight. Pull the 2 ends of the twine through the natural creases of the duck's legs, wrap the ends of the legs and tie tightly. Hang the ducks in a cool dry area for 3 to 5 days.

Preheat the oven to 475 degrees. Rub the ducks with soy sauce and place on a roasting rack. Place in the oven with a baking pan on the lower rack to catch the drippings. Roast for 20 minutes. Reduce the oven temperature to 400 degrees and roast for 15 minutes longer or until pink and cooked to medium. Cool to room temperature. Debone the ducks partially, leaving only the leg bones.

Combine the molasses and vinegar in a small saucepot and cook until reduced by 1/2, skimming the surface occasionally. Preheat the oven to 350 degrees. Heat the vegetable oil in a large ovenproof sauté pan over medium-high heat. Add the ducks skin side down to the sauté pan and sauté until the skin is crisp. Turn the ducks over and pour the molasses glaze over the top. Roast at 350 degrees for 10 to 12 minutes or until done to taste.

To serve, spoon the Dirty Rice and Apple Bacon Cabbage into separate mounds on serving plates. Cut the duck halves into breast and leg portions. Lean the leg portions against the rice. Slice the breast portions and fan around the legs.

What a great Southern dish: peppery dirty rice, braised cabbage and a sweet molasses glaze. It just doesn't get any better than this!

CRAWFISH AND MOLASSES SAUSAGE-STUFFED QUAIL

BLACKBERRY REDUCTION SAUCE

1 tablespoon butter
1/2 cup chopped shallots
leaves of 2 sprigs of thyme
2 bay leaves
1 cup port wine
1 tablespoon balsamic vinegar
2 cups chicken stock (page 197) or canned chicken broth
1 1/2 tablespoons butter, chilled, chopped
1 cup fresh blackberries
kosher salt and cracked black pepper to taste

CRAWFISH AND MOLASSES SAUSAGE-STUFFED QUAIL

8 (3- to 4-ounce) quail
Creole seasoning to taste
16 ounces Molasses Sausage (page 78)
8 ounces crawfish tails
1/4 cup blend of 80% vegetable oil and 20% olive oil
kosher salt and cracked black pepper to taste
1 cup julienned leeks
1 tablespoon butter
Parsnip Potatoes

GARNISH

flat-leaf parsley

■ *Serves 4*

FOR THE SAUCE, melt 1 tablespoon butter in a large saucepot and add the shallots, thyme and bay leaves. Cook, covered, for 5 to 7 minutes. Add the wine and vinegar and stir to deglaze the saucepot. Cook over medium heat until reduced by 1/2. Stir in the chicken stock and cook until reduced to a thick and syrupy sauce.

Whisk in the chilled butter a few pieces at a time, mixing until completely incorporated after each addition. Strain through a fine strainer into a clean saucepot. Stir in the blackberries and season with kosher salt and cracked pepper to taste.

FOR THE QUAIL, debone the quail partially, leaving only the leg bones. Season on all sides with Creole seasoning and place on a work surface. Combine the Molasses Sausage and crawfish tails in a bowl and mix by hand. Shape into 8 balls and place one ball on each quail breast. Roll the quail to enclose the sausage ball. Rub the quail with the oil blend, kosher salt and cracked pepper and place in a roasting pan; insert a meat thermometer into the center. Roast for 30 to 40 minutes or to 160 degrees on the meat thermometer.

Sauté the leeks in the butter in a small sauté pan. Spoon the Parsnip Potatoes into the center of each serving plate and top with the sautéed leeks. Lean 2 quail against the potatoes on each plate. Drizzle with the sauce and garnish with the parsley.

PARSNIP POTATOES

2 to 3 parsnips, peeled
1 1/2 pounds Idaho potatoes,
   peeled, chopped
1/2 cup (1 stick) butter
1/2 cup warm milk
kosher salt and white pepper to taste

FOR THE POTATOES, place the parsnips in a roasting pan and roast at 400 degrees until tender. Let cool enough to handle and purée in a food processor. Measure 1 cup.

Combine the potatoes with water to cover in a saucepot and cook until fork-tender; drain. Mash the potatoes with the 1 cup parsnips in a large mixing bowl. Add the butter and milk and mix until smooth. Season with kosher salt and white pepper.

D E S S E R T S

SUGAR, EGGS, BUTTER, CHOCOLATE, PECANS AND FLOUR ARE

AMONG THE INGREDIENTS USED TO MAKE SUCH CREATIONS

AS WHITE CHOCOLATE BREAD PUDDING OR MOLTEN TURTLE

CAKES. THIS IS THE LAST IMPRESSION OF THE DINING EXPERIENCE, AND

IT SHOULD BE AS MEMORABLE AS ALL THAT HAS COME BEFORE.

CARAMEL IS DECORATIVELY APPLIED TO THE PLATE, A TOUCH OF

RASPBERRY SAUCE AND . . . DONE.

JAMES BEARD HOUSE DINNER

New York, New York

One of Palace Café's greatest honors was the invitation to cook at the
James Beard House in New York City. The James Beard Foundation sponsors awards
that acknowledge restaurants and chefs that strive for excellence. It was
founded to honor James Beard, a true lover of food and good dining.

MENU

Jumbo Shrimp with Tasso, Scallions and Red Pepper Remoulade

Crawfish Bisque with Crispy Okra

Lump Blue Crabmeat with Preserved Mushrooms and Summer Truffle Emulsion

Roasted Pompano on Wilted Baby Spinach with Choupiquette Caviar Cream

White Chocolate Bread Pudding

LA VARENNE AT THE GREENBRIER

White Sulphur Springs, West Virginia

La Varenne Cooking School is based in Paris, France, with a second school
located in White Sulphur Springs, West Virginia at The Greenbrier. The renowned
director, Anne Whalen, and her staff invited Palace Café and Dickie Brennan, who
at the time was the Executive Chef of Palace Café, to instruct one of the
one-week courses they offer. The week culminated in a magnificent seated
dinner featuring the *Flavor of New Orleans* from Palace Café.

MENU

Crabmeat Cheesecake with Pecan Crust

*Duck and Wild Mushroom Roulade
with a Merlot, Creole Mustard and Honey Glaze*

Banana Beignets with Foster Sauce

BANANA BEIGNETS WITH FOSTER SAUCE

FOSTER SAUCE

1 1/2 cups (3 sticks) butter
1 1/2 cups packed dark brown sugar
1 teaspoon ground cinnamon
3/4 cup golden rum
3/4 cup banana liqueur

BEIGNETS

3 cups flour
2 tablespoons baking powder
2 teaspoons sugar
1 teaspoon kosher salt
1 cup water
1 cup milk
1 egg
4 bananas, mashed
vegetable oil for frying
1/2 (1-pound) package
    confectioners' sugar

■ *Serves 4*

FOR THE SAUCE, melt the butter in a small saucepot. Add the brown sugar and cinnamon and mix well. Add the rum and ignite. Allow the flames to subside, then stir in the banana liqueur. Simmer over medium heat for about 2 minutes or until the sauce coats the spoon.

FOR THE BEIGNETS, mix the flour, baking powder, sugar and salt in a medium mixing bowl. Mix the water, milk and egg in a large mixing bowl. Fold in the dry ingredients and mashed bananas.

Heat the oil in a saucepot. Add the batter 1 tablespoon at a time, using a second tablespoon to push the batter off the spoon. Fry for 5 to 7 minutes or until golden brown, turning at least once to ensure even cooking. Remove with a slotted spoon and drain on paper towels.

To serve, ladle the sauce onto serving plates. Place 3 beignets on each plate. Sift the confectioners' sugar over the beignets.

Bananas Foster originated with the Brennan family in the early years of their restaurant days. It has become one of the most widely replicated dishes ever and remains a favorite of ours, especially among our children. It has been an exercise in creativity to evolve the traditional presentation into dishes such as Banana Beignets with Foster Sauce. This recipe takes a simple classic dish and dresses it up with a new look.

BANANA SPLIT CHEESECAKE

CHOCOLATE COOKIE CRUST

2 cups chocolate cookie crumbs
1/2 cup (1 stick) butter, melted, slightly cooled

BANANA FILLING

2 1/4 pounds cream cheese, softened
1 1/4 cups sugar
9 eggs
2 egg yolks
1/4 cup cornstarch
1 cup puréed bananas, about 3 small bananas
3/4 cup banana liqueur
1/4 cup banana extract
1 tablespoon vanilla extract

FRUIT TOPPING

1 cup whipping cream
2 tablespoons sugar
2 cups (1/2-inch) fresh pineapple cubes
2 cups fresh strawberries, cut into quarters
1/2 cup chopped pecans
Caramel Sauce
Chocolate Sauce
10 to 12 maraschino cherries

■ *Serves 10 to 12*

FOR THE CRUST, mix the cookie crumbs and melted butter in a medium bowl. Press the crumbs over the bottom and halfway up the side of a 9-inch springform pan, using the bottom of a glass to pack the crust to an even thickness.

FOR THE FILLING, preheat the oven to 300 degrees. Beat the cream cheese and 1 1/4 cups sugar at medium speed in a mixing bowl until light and fluffy. Beat in the eggs and egg yolks a few at a time. Add the cornstarch, puréed bananas, banana liqueur and extracts and mix until smooth, scraping the side of the bowl with a rubber spatula occasionally.

Pour the filling into the crust, filling to about 1/2 inch from the top of the pan. Bake for 1 1/2 to 2 hours or until the filling is set and light golden brown. Cool on a wire rack. Place on a serving plate and let stand until cool. Remove the side of the pan.

FOR THE TOPPING, whip the cream with the sugar in a mixing bowl until soft peaks form.

To serve, cut the cheesecake into wedges and place on serving plates. Top each slice with the pineapple and strawberries. Sprinkle with the pecans and drizzle with the Caramel Sauce and Chocolate Sauce. Top with whipped cream and a cherry.

The filling for Banana Split Cheesecake can also be prepared in a food processor if the work bowl is large enough to hold all of the ingredients. Combine the filling ingredients and mix at high speed until smooth, scraping the side of the container as needed.

Caramel Sauce

2 cups sugar
1/4 teaspoon fresh lemon juice
2 tablespoons water
1 1/2 cups heavy whipping cream

Chocolate Sauce

1 cup water
1 cup (2 sticks) butter
2/3 cup light corn syrup
1/4 cup Kahlúa
pinch of salt
1 pound semisweet chocolate,
    coarsely chopped

FOR THE CARAMEL SAUCE, combine the sugar, lemon juice and water in a large saucepot. Bring to a boil and cook without stirring until the mixture begins to caramelize on the bottom. Cook until the entire mixture is caramelized, stirring occasionally. Remove from the heat.

Drizzle in the cream in a steady stream, whisking constantly with a long-handled wire whisk; avoid the hot sauce as it foams up during the process. Cool slightly and pour the sauce into a squeeze bottle.

FOR THE CHOCOLATE SAUCE, combine the water, butter, corn syrup, Kahlúa and salt in a saucepot. Bring to a boil and pour over the chocolate in a large mixing bowl. Let stand for 5 to 10 minutes or until the chocolate melts, then whisk until smooth. Cool slightly and pour into a squeeze bottle.

CREOLE CREAM CHEESE CHEESECAKE WITH PRALINE SAUCE

GRAHAM CRACKER CRUST

1 cup (2 sticks) butter
4 cups graham cracker crumbs

FILLING

2 1/2 pounds cream cheese, softened
8 ounces Creole Cream Cheese
    (page 178)
6 eggs
2 cups sugar
2 tablespoons vanilla extract

PRALINE SAUCE

2 cups pecans
2 cups praline liqueur
1 1/2 cups dark corn syrup
1 cup (2 sticks) butter
1/2 cup cornstarch
1 1/2 cups water
1 tablespoon vanilla extract
pinch of salt

■ *Serves 8 to 10*

FOR THE GRAHAM CRACKER CRUST, melt the butter in a small saucepot and pour over the graham cracker crumbs in a large bowl; mix with a wooden spoon. Press 1/4 inch thick over the bottom and halfway up the side of a 9-inch springform pan, using the bottom of a glass to pack firmly.

FOR THE FILLING, preheat the oven to 300 degrees. Combine the cream cheese, Creole Cream Cheese, eggs, sugar and vanilla in a food processor and process until smooth, scraping the side of the processor bowl occasionally. Spoon into the prepared crust. Bake for 2 hours or until set. Cool to room temperature on a wire rack. Chill, covered, in the refrigerator for 6 hours or longer.

FOR THE SAUCE, spread the pecans evenly on a baking sheet. Toast at 300 degrees until golden brown. Combine the liqueur, corn syrup and butter in a saucepot. Bring to a simmer.

Combine the cornstarch with the water in a small bowl. Whisk a small amount of the hot liqueur mixture into the cornstarch paste, then whisk the cornstarch paste into the hot liqueur. Cook until the sauce thickens, whisking constantly. Stir in the pecans, vanilla and salt. Cool to room temperature.

To serve, place the cheesecake on a serving plate and remove the side of the pan. Cut into slices and spoon the sauce over the slices.

Creole Cream Cheese is a New Orleans specialty that has the texture of thick sour cream and a slightly tarter taste than regular cream cheese. We've included the recipe on page 178, and it's easy to make. But, remember, it has to be made at least three to four days in advance.

STRAWBERRY SHORTCAKE

MARINATED STRAWBERRIES

2 cups sugar
1 tablespoon balsamic vinegar
4 pints strawberries, stemmed

SHORTCAKE

3 cups all-purpose flour
1 cup cake flour
1 cup sugar
2 tablespoons baking powder
1/8 teaspoon salt
1/2 cup (1 stick) butter, chilled, chopped
1 1/2 cups buttermilk
1 pint (2 cups) whipping cream

GARNISH

1/4 cup confectioners' sugar
reserved strawberries

■ *Serves 8*

FOR THE STRAWBERRIES, mix the sugar and balsamic vinegar in a mixing bowl. Reserve 8 strawberries for garnish, quarter the remaining strawberries and add them to the sugar mixture. Marinate in the refrigerator for 1 hour or longer to allow the juices to accumulate.

FOR THE SHORTCAKE, preheat the oven to 325 degrees. Combine the all-purpose flour, cake flour, sugar, baking powder and salt in a medium mixing bowl and whisk to mix well. Cut in the butter with 2 knives to make crumbs the size of small peas. Add the buttermilk and mix well; squeeze by hand into a slightly wet and sticky dough.

Knead lightly on a floured surface and pat 1 inch thick. Cut 3-inch circles with a cutter or the rim of a large glass dipped in flour. Place on a baking sheet lined with baking parchment. Bake for 20 to 25 minutes or until golden brown.

Beat the whipping cream in a mixing bowl until soft peaks form. Split the shortcakes into halves horizontally. Spoon the accumulated strawberry juice onto the cut sides of the shortcakes. Place the bottom halves on serving plates and top with the marinated strawberries and a dollop of whipped cream. Replace the tops of the shortcakes. Garnish with confectioners' sugar and the reserved strawberries.

SEASONAL FRUIT COBBLER

FRUIT FILLING

6 cups fresh seasonal fruit
2 cups sugar
1 cup all-purpose flour
2 tablespoons butter, melted, slightly
    cooled

FLAKY CRUST

2 1/2 cups all-purpose flour
2 1/2 cups cake flour
1/4 cup sugar
1 teaspoon salt
1 egg yolk
1 cup (2 sticks) butter, chopped,
    chilled
1/2 cup shortening
3/4 cup ice water
1/4 cup milk
2 tablespoons sugar

■ *Serves 6 to 8*

FOR THE FILLING, peel and slice fruit other than berries. Toss the fruit with the sugar, flour and butter in a bowl, coating well. Chill, covered, in the refrigerator until ready to use.

FOR THE CRUST, mix the all-purpose flour, cake flour, 1/4 cup sugar and salt in a large stainless steel bowl. Stir in the egg yolk. Cut in the butter and shortening with a pastry cutter or 2 knives to make crumbs the size of small peas.

Add 1/3 of the ice water at a time and squeeze together by hand to make a dough that is sticky and moist but not wet. Do not overmix the dough; having small pieces of butter visible in the dough is fine. Shape into two equal portions, wrap in plastic wrap and chill for 2 hours or longer.

Place one portion of dough on a floured surface and sprinkle with a small amount of flour. Roll into a rectangle 1/4 inch thick and large enough to cover the bottom and sides of a greased 8×10-inch baking dish; flip the dough several times while rolling to ensure an even thickness. Sprinkle the rolling surface and pin with additional flour if necessary to prevent sticking. Roll the dough around the rolling pin then unroll it into the dish. Pat gently into the dish and trim the edges. Chill slightly in the refrigerator.

To assemble and bake, preheat the oven to 350 degrees. Spoon the filling into the prepared dish. Roll the remaining dough portion into a rectangle slightly larger than the baking dish using the same technique. Place over the filling and trim or tuck under and flute the edges. Brush with the milk and sprinkle with 2 tablespoons sugar. Cut 3 or 4 X-shaped vents at even intervals in the top. Bake for 35 to 40 minutes or until the crust is golden brown and the filling is bubbly.

We always use the freshest seasonal fruit and recommend that you use what is best in your area. Some of our favorite combinations for Seasonal Fruit Cobbler are blueberry and peach, apple and cherry, strawberry and rhubarb, and blueberry and blackberry.

CAFÉ AU LAIT CRÈME BRÛLÉE

INGREDIENTS

1 quart heavy whipping cream
1/3 cup coarsely ground espresso
   beans
3/4 cup sugar
11 egg yolks
1 tablespoon vanilla extract
1 tablespoon turbinado sugar or raw
   sugar

■ *Serves 10*

Preheat the oven to 225 degrees. Combine the whipping cream and ground espresso beans in a heavy small saucepot and bring to a boil. Remove from the heat and stir in the sugar until dissolved. Whisk the egg yolks and vanilla gently in a large bowl. Whisk in the warm cream mixture gradually. Pour through a fine strainer into another bowl; check for coffee grains and re-strain if necessary.

Pour the mixture into a 9×12-inch baking dish. Bake for 1 to 1 1/2 hours or until the custard is set enough to jiggle as a unit when the dish is tapped; the center should still be slightly liquid. Cool to room temperature and chill, covered, in the refrigerator for 1 to 2 hours or until set.

Sprinkle with the turbinado sugar. Caramelize the sugar with a small kitchen torch or brûlée iron, keeping the flame moving to create a uniform medium amber color. Serve with your favorite cookies or fresh seasonal fruits.

You can bake Café au Lait Crème Brûlée in individual dishes if you prefer. Fill the dishes to about 1/4 inch below the rims of the dishes and bake until the custard jiggles as a unit when the dishes are tapped.

WHITE CHOCOLATE
CRÈME BRÛLÉE

INGREDIENTS

1 quart heavy whipping cream
8 ounces white chocolate, coarsely
    chopped
1 cup egg yolks, about 8 egg yolks
2/3 cup sugar
2 tablespoons vanilla extract
sugar for topping

GARNISH

fresh seasonal fruit

■ *Serves 6 to 8*

Preheat the oven to 225 degrees. Bring the cream to a simmer in a heavy saucepot. Remove from the heat and add the white chocolate pieces. Let stand for 3 to 5 minutes, then whisk until smooth.

Whisk the egg yolks, 2/3 cup sugar and vanilla in a mixing bowl. Add the white chocolate mixture, scraping from the saucepot with a rubber spatula; whisk until smooth. Pour into a 9×9-inch baking dish or fill individual baking dishes 3/4 full. Bake for 1 hour or until the center jiggles slightly when the dish is tapped. Cool to room temperature and chill in the refrigerator for 1 to 2 hours or until set.

Sprinkle the top with additional sugar. Caramelize the sugar with a small kitchen torch or brûlée iron, keeping the flame moving to create a uniform medium amber color. Garnish with fresh seasonal fruit.

The subtle hint of white chocolate in this crème brûlée makes all the difference. Try substituting dark chocolate, if that's what you prefer.

WHITE CHOCOLATE
BREAD PUDDING

WHITE CHOCOLATE
BREAD PUDDING

6 cups heavy whipping cream
2 cups milk
1 cup sugar
20 ounces white chocolate, broken
    into small pieces
4 eggs
15 egg yolks
1 (24-inch) loaf stale French bread
    or fresh French bread that has
    been sliced and dried in a
    275-degree oven

WHITE CHOCOLATE
GANACHE

1/2 cup heavy whipping cream
8 ounces white chocolate, broken
    into small pieces

GARNISH

1 ounce dark chocolate, shaved or
    grated

■ *Serves 12*

FOR THE PUDDING, combine the whipping cream, milk and sugar in a large heavy saucepot and mix well. Bring to a boil then remove from the heat. Add the white chocolate pieces and let stand for several minutes or until the chocolate melts; stir until smooth.

Whisk the eggs and egg yolks in a large mixing bowl. Whisk in the warm chocolate mixture in a slow steady stream; scrape the saucepot with a rubber spatula to remove all the chocolate.

Preheat the oven to 350 degrees. Cut the French bread into thin slices and place in a 9×12-inch metal baking pan. Pour half the chocolate mixture over the bread and let stand for about 5 minutes. Press the bread into the chocolate mixture with a rubber spatula or fingers to saturate well. Pour the remaining chocolate mixture over the bread and stir to mix well.

Cover the pan with foil and bake for 1 hour. Remove the foil and bake for 30 minutes longer or until golden brown. Cool to room temperature and chill, covered, in the refrigerator for 6 to 8 hours or until set.

FOR THE GANACHE, bring the whipping cream to a boil in a small saucepan. Remove from the heat and add the white chocolate pieces. Let stand until the chocolate melts and stir until smooth.

Loosen the pudding from the sides of the pan with a knife and invert onto a work surface. Cut into squares, then cut the squares diagonally into triangles. Place the triangles on a baking sheet and reheat at 275 degrees for 15 minutes or until warm.

To serve, place the pudding triangles on serving plates and top with the ganache. Garnish with dark chocolate shavings.

W̶hite Chocolate Bread Pudding is a signature dish requested for many of the special menus that we serve around the country. It can be spooned right out of the pan while it's still warm to serve, as well as prepared in advance and reheated as we've done in this recipe.

CREOLE CREAM CHEESE ICE CREAM

INGREDIENTS

4 cups (1 quart) heavy cream
2¹/2 cups milk
1 cup sugar
16 egg yolks
1¹/2 cups sugar
1 cup Creole Cream Cheese (below)

■ *Makes about ¹/2 gallon*

Combine the cream, milk and 1 cup sugar in a heavy saucepot. Bring to a simmer over low heat. Whisk the egg yolks and 1¹/2 cups sugar in a mixing bowl. Whisk a small amount of the hot cream into the egg yolk mixture, then whisk the egg yolk mixture into the hot cream. Remove from the heat and whisk in the Creole Cream Cheese.

Strain into a bowl and cool to room temperature. Pour into an ice cream freezer container and freeze using the manufacturer's instructions.

CREOLE CREAM CHEESE

INGREDIENTS

8 cups (¹/2 gallon) skim milk
12 drops liquid rennin, or
    ¹/4 rennin tablet
¹/4 cup buttermilk

■ *Makes about 2 cups*

Heat the skim milk to 80 to 90 degrees in a saucepot, using a thermometer to determine the temperature. Stir the rennin into the buttermilk in a bowl; if using tablet rennin, stir until the tablet dissolves. Add the buttermilk mixture to the skim milk and mix well.

Pour into a clean container and let stand, uncovered, in a place that is not in a direct flow of hot or cold air for 24 to 30 hours to curdle.

Pour the curds into a large strainer lined with cheesecloth and placed over a bowl. Place in the refrigerator to drain for 2 days or until liquid no longer drains from the curds; discard the liquid. Store the Creole Cream Cheese in the refrigerator for up to 1 week.

Creole Cream Cheese is an old Brennan family favorite. It's slightly more tart than regular cream cheese. Dick Brennan remembers the milkman delivering Creole Cream Cheese, along with the other dairy products, to his home regularly as a child. His mother would sprinkle sugar and fresh fruit over it and serve it for breakfast.

Since it's generally not available outside of Louisiana, we've included a method for making it with rennin. Rennin is an enzyme that curdles milk and is available in most supermarkets in tablet, liquid or powdered form.

BLACKOUT CAKE

CHOCOLATE PUDDING

2/3 cup sugar
1/2 cup all-purpose flour
2 cups cold milk
4 egg yolks
pinch of salt
3 ounces unsweetened chocolate
2 tablespoons butter
1 1/2 teaspoons vanilla extract

DEVIL'S FOOD CAKE

1 cup sugar
1/2 cup buttermilk
2/3 cup baking cocoa
2 cups cake flour
1 teaspoon baking soda
1/2 teaspoon baking powder
1/2 teaspoon salt
1/2 cup buttermilk
1 teaspoon vanilla extract
1/2 cup (1 stick) butter, softened
1 cup sugar
2 eggs
Nocello Simple Syrup (page 183)

■ *Serves 12*

FOR THE PUDDING, combine the sugar, flour, milk, egg yolks and salt in a medium stainless steel mixing bowl and whisk until smooth. Set the bowl over a saucepot of simmering water. Cook over medium-high heat for 10 to 15 minutes or until the mixture has a consistency slightly thinner than pudding, whisking constantly to prevent lumps from forming. Remove from the heat and add the chocolate, butter and vanilla, stirring until the chocolate and butter melt and the mixture is smooth. Cover with plastic wrap and chill in the refrigerator for 2 hours or until set.

FOR THE CAKE, preheat the oven to 350 degrees. Combine 1 cup sugar, 1/2 cup buttermilk and the baking cocoa in a bowl and whisk to form a thick paste. Sift the cake flour, baking soda, baking powder and salt together. Combine 1/2 cup buttermilk and the vanilla in a small bowl.

Cream the butter and 1 cup sugar in a mixing bowl until light and fluffy. Beat in the eggs one at a time. Add the cocoa and buttermilk paste and beat until smooth. Add the sifted dry ingredients 1/3 at a time, alternating with the buttermilk and vanilla mixture and mixing well after each addition.

Spoon the batter evenly into 2 greased and floured round 9-inch cake pans and smooth the tops. Bake for 30 minutes or until a wooden pick or cake tester inserted in the center comes out clean. Cool on wire racks.

To assemble, slice each cake layer horizontally with a serrated knife, making 4 layers. Reserve the smoothest layer for the top of the cake and the least regular for crumbs.

Moisten one of the remaining layers with 1/3 of the simple syrup using a pastry brush. Place on a cake plate. Spread about 1/4 of the cooled pudding about 1/2 inch thick over the layer. Place a second layer on the first; moisten with the simple syrup and spread with the pudding. Top with the reserved even layer and repeat the process. Frost the side with the remaining pudding.

Grind the remaining reserved layer into crumbs in a food processor. Pat gently over the top and side of the cake. Chill, covered, for up to 12 hours before slicing and serving.

HONEY'S CARROT CAKE

CARROT CAKE

2 cups all-purpose flour, sifted
2 teaspoons baking powder
2 teaspoons baking soda
1 teaspoon salt
2 cups sugar
1 1/2 cups vegetable oil
4 eggs
4 to 5 cups finely grated carrots
4 cups finely chopped pecans
2 tablespoons vanilla extract

CREAM CHEESE FROSTING

16 ounces cream cheese, softened
1/2 cup (1 stick) butter, softened
2 teaspoons vanilla extract
1 1/2 cups confectioners' sugar

■ *Serves 12*

FOR THE CAKE, preheat the oven to 325 degrees. Whisk the flour, baking powder, baking soda and salt in a medium mixing bowl. Combine the sugar and vegetable oil in a large mixing bowl and beat until smooth. Beat in the eggs one at a time. Add the dry ingredients gradually, mixing well after each addition. Stir in the carrots, pecans and vanilla.

Spoon into 3 greased round 9-inch cake pans. Bake for 45 minutes. Cool in the pans for 10 minutes, then remove to a wire rack to cool completely.

FOR THE FROSTING, combine the cream cheese and butter in a mixing bowl and beat until light and fluffy. Add the vanilla and confectioners' sugar and beat until smooth.

Frost the tops and sides of the three layers. Stack them on a cake plate and smooth the frosting on the top and sides of the layered cake.

We don't usually name dishes for people at Palace Café, but Honey's Carrot Cake is special. The recipe is actually from Dickie's and Lauren's grandmother on the Trist side—their mom's mom, Honey. She made this cake regularly, and the recipe is used by the restaurant in its original form.

MOCHA DOBERGE CAKE

MOCHA BUTTERCREAM

1 cup egg whites, about 8
2 cups sugar
1 tablespoon instant coffee granules
3 cups (6 sticks) butter, softened

CHOCOLATE SPONGE CAKE

1 3/4 cups cake flour
1/4 cup baking cocoa
8 eggs
1 1/2 cups sugar
1 teaspoon vanilla extract
1/2 cup (1 stick) butter, melted,
   slightly cooled
Nocello Simple Syrup

CHOCOLATE GANACHE

8 ounces semisweet chocolate
1 cup heavy cream

■ *Serves 12*

FOR THE BUTTERCREAM, combine the egg whites, sugar and coffee granules in a stainless steel bowl. Set the bowl over a saucepot of simmering water. Cook until the sugar dissolves, stirring constantly. Remove from the heat and beat with an electric mixer until stiff peaks form. Add the butter very gradually, beating constantly until all the butter has been incorporated and the buttercream is smooth and satiny.

FOR THE CAKE, preheat the oven to 350 degrees. Sift the cake flour and baking cocoa into a small mixing bowl. Combine the eggs, sugar and vanilla in a large mixing bowl. Beat with an electric mixer for 10 to 15 minutes or until light. Fold in the sifted ingredients 1/4 at a time, bringing the batter from the bottom of the bowl to the top with a rubber spatula in a circular motion in order to avoid deflating the egg white mixture. Fold in the butter in the same manner.

Spoon evenly into 2 or 4 greased and floured 9-inch cake pans and smooth the tops. Bake for 20 to 30 minutes or until a wooden pick or cake tester inserted in the center comes out clean. Cool in the pans for 10 minutes, then remove to a wire rack to cool completely.

To assemble the cake, slice the layers horizontally into 2 even layers with a serrated knife to make 4 layers if baked in 2 pans. Moisten the cake layers generously with the Nocello Simple Syrup using a pastry brush. Spread the buttercream over the tops and sides of the layers and stack on a cake plate, using the smoothest layer for the top; smooth the buttercream over the side. Chill, covered, in the refrigerator to set the buttercream.

FOR THE GANACHE, chop the chocolate into medium pieces. Bring the cream to a simmer in a heavy saucepot. Remove from the heat and add the chocolate. Let stand for 5 to 10 minutes or until the chocolate melts; whisk until smooth. Cool slightly.

Pour the ganache over the chilled cake and smooth over the top and side with a rubber spatula or flat knife. Chill, covered, for 1 hour or until the ganache is set.

NOCELLO SIMPLE SYRUP

1/2 cup water
1/2 cup sugar
1/2 cup Nocello walnut liqueur

FOR THE SYRUP, combine the water, sugar and liqueur in a small saucepan and bring to a simmer over medium heat. Cook until the sugar dissolves, stirring constantly. Cool slightly.

Clockwise from top: Mocha Doberge Cake; Molten Turtle Cakes (page 184); Mississippi Mud Pie (page 185)

MOLTEN TURTLE CAKES

INGREDIENTS

8 ounces semisweet chocolate
1 cup sugar
2 1/2 cups (5 sticks) butter
1 1/2 cups all-purpose flour
1/4 cup baking cocoa
2 teaspoons baking powder
7 eggs
12 soft caramel candies
Chocolate Sauce (page 169)
Caramel Sauce (page 169)

■ *Serves 12*

Photograph for this recipe is on page 183.

Chop the chocolate into small pieces and mix with the sugar in a large mixing bowl. Melt the butter in a saucepot and heat until bubbly. Pour over the chocolate and let stand for 5 minutes to melt the chocolate. Mix with a mixer at low speed until smooth.

Whisk the flour, baking cocoa and baking powder in a mixing bowl. Add to the chocolate mixture gradually, mixing well after each addition. Beat in the eggs one at a time at low speed, then beat at high speed for 10 minutes.

Preheat the oven to 350 degrees. Coat ceramic ramekins generously with nonstick cooking spray. Fill the ramekins halfway with the batter and drop a caramel candy into each ramekin, covering completely with the batter. Place on a baking sheet.

Bake for 15 to 18 minutes or until set on the outer edge but liquid in the center; cakes should jiggle as a unit when the ramekins are shaken. You may want to bake one ramekin as a test cake and adjust your baking time accordingly.

To serve, loosen the cakes gently from the sides of the ramekins with a knife and invert onto serving plates; tap or shake gently to release the cakes. Drizzle the plates with the Chocolate Sauce and Caramel Sauce.

You may bake this batter as soon as it is mixed or store it in the refrigerator for several days before baking.

The Chocolate Sauce and Caramel Sauce used to drizzle over the serving plates are great to keep on hand for different desserts. Store them in microwave-safe squeeze bottles in the refrigerator and microwave them for a few seconds before each use.

MISSISSIPPI MUD PIE

CHOCOLATE COOKIE CRUST

3 1/2 cups Oreo cookie crumbs or other chocolate wafer crumbs
1/4 cup (1/2 stick) butter, melted

FILLING

4 cups heavy whipping cream
2 teaspoons vanilla extract
1/3 cup sugar
2 cups heavy whipping cream
1 1/2 pounds semisweet chocolate, coarsely chopped
1 ounce unflavored gelatin
5 1/2 ounces amaretto

■ *Serves 6 to 8*

Photograph for this recipe is on page 183.

FOR THE CRUST, preheat the oven to 350 degrees. Mix the cookie crumbs and melted butter in a large bowl. Press firmly over the bottom and up the side of a 9-inch springform pan, using the bottom of a glass to pack the crumbs firmly. Chill for 30 minutes. Bake for 10 minutes. Chill until ready to fill.

FOR THE FILLING, combine 4 cups whipping cream and vanilla in a medium mixing bowl. Beat with a mixer until soft peaks form. Add the sugar and beat until firm peaks form.

Bring 2 cups whipping cream to a simmer in a saucepan. Pour over the chocolate in a stainless steel bowl and let stand for 5 minutes to melt the chocolate for the ganache. Whisk until smooth. Hold at room temperature.

Bring about 1 inch water to a simmer in a medium saucepot. Sprinkle the gelatin over the amaretto in a stainless steel bowl and let stand for several minutes to soften. Place the bowl over the simmering water and cook until the gelatin dissolves, stirring constantly. Hold over low heat.

To assemble the pie:
Layer 1—spread 1 cup of the chocolate ganache over the bottom of the chilled pie crust. Freeze for 30 minutes.
Layer 2—fold 2 tablespoons of the amaretto gelatin, 2/3 cup of the whipped cream and 3/4 cup of the chocolate ganache together in a bowl. Spread over the first pie layer. Freeze for 30 minutes.
Layer 3—fold 2 tablespoons of the amaretto gelatin, 1 cup of the whipped cream and 1/2 cup of the chocolate ganache together in a bowl. Spread over the second pie layer. Freeze for 30 minutes.
Layer 4—fold 2 tablespoons of the amaretto gelatin, 1 3/4 cups of the whipped cream and 1/3 cup of the chocolate ganache together in a bowl. Spread over the third pie layer. Freeze for 30 minutes.
Layer 5—fold 2 tablespoons of the amaretto gelatin, 2 1/3 cups of the whipped cream and 1/4 cup of the chocolate ganache together in a bowl. Spread over the fourth pie layer. Freeze for 30 minutes.

Spoon the remaining whipped cream into a pastry bag fitted with a star tip and pipe as desired over the top and edges. Chill or freeze the pie until time to serve.

PECAN PIE

FLAKY PIE CRUST

2 1/2 cups all-purpose flour
2 1/2 cups cake flour
1/4 cup sugar
1 teaspoon salt
1 egg yolk
1 cup (2 sticks) butter, chopped,
    chilled
1/2 cup shortening
3/4 cup ice water

PECAN FILLING

2 cups sugar
2 cups dark corn syrup
8 eggs
2 tablespoons vanilla extract
1 cup (2 sticks) butter, melted,
    slightly cooled
2 cups pecans or pecan pieces

■ *Makes 2 pies*

FOR THE CRUST, mix the all-purpose flour, cake flour, sugar and salt in a large stainless steel bowl. Stir in the egg yolk. Cut in the cold butter and shortening with a pastry cutter or 2 knives to make crumbs the size of small peas.

Add 1/3 of the ice water at a time and squeeze together by hand to make a dough that is sticky and slightly moist but not wet. Do not overmix the dough; having small pieces of butter visible in the dough is fine. Shape into two equal portions, wrap in plastic wrap and chill for 2 hours or longer.

Place one portion of the dough at a time on a floured surface and sprinkle with a small amount of flour. Roll into a circle 3 inches larger than the top of an 8-inch pie pan; flip the dough several times while rolling to ensure an even thickness. Sprinkle the rolling surface and rolling pin with additional flour if necessary to prevent sticking. Roll the dough around the rolling pin then unroll it into the pie pan. Pat gently into the pie pan and trim the edges, patching any tears with the trimmings if necessary. Flute the edge. Repeat the process with the remaining dough. Chill slightly in the refrigerator.

FOR THE FILLING, preheat the oven to 375 degrees. Combine the sugar, corn syrup, eggs and vanilla in a large mixing bowl and whisk by hand or beat with a mixer until smooth. Add the butter gradually, mixing constantly.

Sprinkle 1 cup of the pecans into each pie shell. Pour the filling over the pecans, filling to within 1/2 inch of the top. Bake for 20 minutes. Reduce the oven temperature to 350 degrees and bake for 40 minutes longer or until set.

After years of recipe testing and tweaking, here it is—the absolute best recipe for great no-frills pecan pie. The only thing finer than a warm slice of this classic, extra-buttery pecan pie is one topped with a scoop of homemade vanilla bean ice cream!

FIG PECAN TART

FIG COMPOTE

1 pound fresh figs
1/2 cup sugar
2 tablespoons port or madeira

TART CRUST

1/2 cup (1 stick) butter, softened
1/4 cup sugar
1 egg
1 teaspoon vanilla extract
1 1/2 cups all-purpose flour

FILLING

3 eggs, beaten
1/2 cup sugar
2 tablespoons butter, melted
1/4 cup dark corn syrup
1 teaspoon vanilla extract
1 1/4 cups chopped pecans

CHOCOLATE GANACHE

1 cup heavy cream
8 ounces semisweet chocolate,
  chopped

■ *Serves 6 to 8*

FOR THE FIG COMPOTE, wash the figs, discarding the stems. Combine with the sugar and wine in a small saucepot and simmer over medium heat for 45 minutes or until thickened. Cool to room temperature. Store unused portions in the refrigerator.

FOR THE CRUST, cream the butter and sugar in a mixing bowl until light and fluffy. Add the egg and vanilla and mix until smooth. Add the flour and beat until the mixture forms a ball that cleans the bottom of the mixing bowl. Wrap in plastic wrap and chill for 1 hour.

Place the dough on a lightly floured surface and roll with a lightly floured rolling pin into a circle slightly larger than a 9-inch tart pan. Place in the tart pan and press evenly into the pan with floured fingers. Flute the edge.

FOR THE FILLING, preheat the oven to 350 degrees. Combine the eggs, sugar, butter, corn syrup and vanilla in a mixing bowl and mix well. Stir in 3/4 cup fig compote and pecans. Spoon into the prepared pie shell.

Bake for 45 minutes or until set. Chill, covered, in the refrigerator until time to spread with the ganache.

FOR THE GANACHE, bring the cream to a simmer in a heavy saucepot. Pour over the chocolate in a mixing bowl and let stand for 5 minutes or until melted. Whisk to mix well.

To serve, pour the warm ganache over the tart and spread evenly with a rubber spatula. Chill, covered, until serving time.

You can also make the Fig Pecan Tart with dried figs. Cut 1/2 pound of dried figs into quarters and mix with 1/4 cup sugar and 1/2 cup wine in a small saucepot. Simmer over medium heat until the figs are tender and then purée them to use in the recipe.

LEMON FLAN TARTLETS

SUGAR CRUST

1 cup (2 sticks) butter, softened
1/2 cup sugar
3 cups all-purpose flour
1 egg

LEMON FLAN FILLING

8 ounces cream cheese, softened
1/2 cup sugar
1 tablespoon finely grated lemon
     zest
1/2 cup strained lemon juice, about
     3 lemons
2 eggs

LEMON CURD

5 egg yolks
2/3 cup sugar
1/2 cup (1 stick) butter
1/2 cup strained lemon juice, about
     3 lemons
1 1/2 teaspoons finely grated lemon
     zest

■ *Serves 8 to 12*

FOR THE CRUST, cream the butter and sugar in a mixing bowl until light and fluffy. Add the flour and egg and beat just until mixed; do not overmix. Wrap with plastic wrap and chill in the refrigerator for 30 minutes.

Preheat the oven to 350 degrees. Place the dough on a lightly floured surface and roll 1/8 inch thick. Cut out circles slightly larger than your tartlet pans with a floured knife or cutter dipped in flour. Press the circles gently into the tartlet pans. Chill for 10 minutes. Bake for 25 minutes or until golden brown. Cool to room temperature.

FOR THE FILLING, combine the cream cheese and sugar in a mixing bowl and beat until very smooth, scraping the side of the bowl with a rubber spatula occasionally. Add the lemon zest, lemon juice and eggs; mix until smooth. Chill, covered, until ready to use.

To bake the tartlets, preheat the oven to 275 degrees. Fill the baked tartlet shells with the filling. Bake for 15 minutes or until set.

FOR THE LEMON CURD, combine the egg yolks, sugar, butter, lemon juice and lemon zest in a heavy saucepot and cook over low heat until thickened, stirring constantly. Cool slightly.

To serve, spoon the warm lemon curd onto serving plates and place one tart in the center of each plate.

Everyone who works the pastry station at Palace Café knows that Dickie loves lemon desserts! These tartlets take a little longer to make than some of our other desserts, but the elegant presentation is well worth the time and effort. The tartlet shells, filling and curd can all be made in advance. Just chill, covered, until ready to use. Then, when ready to serve, fill the shells, bake for 15 minutes, and warm the lemon curd over low heat.

LEMON BARS

LEMON BAR CRUST

1 1/2 cups all-purpose flour
1/4 cup confectioners' sugar
1/8 teaspoon salt
1/2 cup (1 stick) butter, chilled, chopped
1/2 teaspoon vanilla extract

LEMON FILLING

5 eggs
2 cups sugar
1 cup lemon juice
3 tablespoons all-purpose flour
3 tablespoons lemon zest

GARNISH

1/4 cup confectioners' sugar

■ *Makes about 2 dozen*

FOR THE CRUST, preheat the oven to 350 degrees. Line a 9×9-inch baking pan with foil and spray with nonstick cooking spray. Combine the flour, confectioners' sugar, salt, butter and vanilla in a food processor and process until well mixed. Press evenly over the bottom of the prepared baking pan. Bake for 20 to 30 minutes or until golden brown.

FOR THE FILLING, combine the eggs, sugar, lemon juice and flour in a mixing bowl and whisk until smooth. Strain into a clean bowl and stir in the lemon zest. Pour over the prepared crust.

Bake for 20 minutes or until set. Cool on a wire rack for 8 hours or longer. Cut into 1×3-inch bars. Sift the confectioners' sugar over the tops to garnish.

Dessert doesn't get much more Southern than this! These lemon bars are easy to make and are the perfect way to finish a casual summer supper. They're also one of Chef Gus Martin's all-time favorite desserts!

ET CETERA

THE DOORS ARE CLOSED, AND THE STAFF RELAXES. WAITSTAFF

LOOSEN THEIR TIES, AND COOKS LOOK OVER THEIR STATIONS

AND REVIEW WHAT NEEDS TO BE REPLACED BEFORE THE NEXT

SERVICE BEGINS. STOCKPOTS ARE CHECKED, SEASONINGS AND

SEASONING BLENDS ARE REPLENISHED. THERE'S A CERTAIN SENSE

OF SATISFACTION THAT COMES FROM PROVIDING A GREAT MEAL

AND, WE ALL HOPE, A GREAT EXPERIENCE FOR THOSE WHO HAVE

JUST DINED AT PALACE CAFÉ.

AU POIVRE SAUCE

INGREDIENTS

5 pints duck stock (page 197)
1 tablespoon butter
3 shallots, chopped
1 tablespoon black pepper
2 tablespoons brandy
1/2 cup cream
1 tablespoon butter, chopped, chilled
kosher salt to taste

■ *Makes about 1¹/2 cups*

Cook the duck stock in a saucepot until it is reduced to 1 cup. Melt 1 tablespoon butter in a large sauté pan over medium heat and add the shallots. Cook for 1 minute. Add the pepper and brandy. Ignite the brandy and allow the flames to subside.

Add the reduced duck stock to the shallot mixture, mix well and bring to a boil. Reduce the heat and stir in the cream. Simmer until the sauce thickens slightly. Remove from the heat and whisk in the chilled butter. Season with kosher salt and keep warm.

BÉARNAISE SAUCE

INGREDIENTS

2 cups (4 sticks) butter
1 cup chopped tarragon
1 tablespoon chopped shallots
1 cup red wine vinegar
1 teaspoon cracked black pepper
5 egg yolks
1/4 cup water
1/2 teaspoon salt
cracked black pepper and kosher
    salt to taste

■ *Makes about 2¹/2 cups*

Melt the butter in a sauté pan over low heat and skim off the cloudy foam. Scoop the clear butter off the milk solids which sink to the bottom of the pan. Cool slightly.

Combine the tarragon, shallots, wine vinegar and 1 teaspoon cracked pepper in a saucepan and cook over medium heat until the vinegar evaporates. Cool to room temperature.

Whisk the egg yolks, water and 1/2 teaspoon salt in a double boiler or metal bowl placed over a saucepan of boiling water. Cook until the mixture is about three times the original volume and pale yellow, whisking constantly. Remove from the heat and whisk in the warm clarified butter gradually until the sauce is pale yellow, thick and creamy. Stir in the reduced vinegar mixture. Adjust the seasoning with cracked pepper and kosher salt to taste.

CHORON SAUCE

INGREDIENTS

2 tomatoes, coarsely chopped
1 dried shallot, chopped
1/2 cup red wine
1 tablespoon rice wine vinegar
2 teaspoons fresh or dried tarragon
5 egg yolks
1 teaspoon Tabasco sauce
1 teaspoon lemon juice
2 tablespoons water
1 pound butter, clarified
kosher salt and white pepper to taste

■ *Makes about 2 cups*

Sauté the tomatoes with the shallot, red wine, wine vinegar and tarragon in a saucepan over medium heat until most of the liquid has evaporated. Cool to room temperature.

Whisk the egg yolks, Tabasco sauce, lemon juice and water in a double boiler or metal bowl atop a saucepan of boiling water. Cook until the mixture is almost triple the original volume and pale yellow, whisking rapidly; remove from the heat during the cooking period if necessary to prevent the eggs from scrambling.

Remove from the heat and whisk in the clarified butter gradually until thick and creamy. Stir in the tomato reduction and season with kosher salt and white pepper. Keep warm until serving time.

HOLLANDAISE SAUCE

INGREDIENTS

2 cups (4 sticks) butter
5 egg yolks
2 tablespoons white wine
4 dashes of Tabasco sauce
juice of 1 1/2 lemons
1 tablespoon finely chopped parsley
kosher salt and white pepper to taste

■ *Makes about 2 1/2 cups*

Clarify the butter by melting it in a sauté pan; skim off and discard the foam. Spoon the clear butter off the milk solids which settle to the bottom.

Whisk the egg yolks, white wine, Tabasco sauce, lemon juice and parsley in a double boiler or metal bowl placed over a saucepan of boiling water. Cook until the mixture is almost triple the original volume and pale yellow; remove from the heat during the cooking period if necessary to avoid scrambling the eggs. Remove from the heat and add the clarified butter very gradually, whisking until thick and creamy. Season with kosher salt and white pepper.

CREOLE MEUNIÈRE SAUCE

INGREDIENTS

1 lemon, peeled, cut into quarters
1/2 cup Worcestershire sauce
1/2 cup Crystal hot sauce
1/4 cup heavy whipping cream
2 cups (4 sticks) butter, chilled, cut
   into small pieces
kosher salt and white pepper to taste

■ *Makes about 3 cups*

Combine the lemon, Worcestershire sauce and hot sauce in a heavy saucepot. Cook over medium heat until the liquid is thick and syrupy, whisking constantly. Whisk in the whipping cream and reduce the heat to low.

Add the butter one piece at a time, mixing until the butter has been completely incorporated after each addition. Remove from the heat and stir until smooth. Season with kosher salt and white pepper. Strain through a fine strainer into a saucepot and keep warm.

ROASTED TOMATO SAUCE

INGREDIENTS

3 or 4 medium tomatoes
vegetable oil
1/2 cup Tabasco sauce
2 cups white wine
2 shallots, minced
3/4 cup heavy cream
3 cups (6 sticks) butter, chilled,
   chopped

■ *Makes 7 to 8 cups*

Core the tomatoes and cut into halves. Rub the skins with a small amount of vegetable oil and make a slit in the skin of each half. Arrange cut side down in a baking pan and roast at 400 degrees until the skins blister. Cool, remove the skins, squeeze out the seeds and chop the tomatoes.

Combine the Tabasco sauce, white wine and shallots in a medium saucepot and cook for 20 minutes or until syrupy. Add the roasted tomatoes and cook until the juices evaporate. Stir in the cream and simmer until the sauce is thick enough to coat the spoon. Whisk in the butter a few pieces at a time, mixing well after each addition. Keep warm.

BASIL OIL

INGREDIENTS

1/2 cup basil stems
1 cup olive oil
1/2 cup julienned fresh basil

■ *Makes 1 1/2 cups*

Combine the basil stems with the olive oil in a small saucepot and heat over medium heat until heated through. Remove from the heat and let cool to room temperature. Discard the stems, add the julienned basil and purée in a food processor.

CRYSTAL BEURRE BLANC

INGREDIENTS

1 cup Crystal hot sauce
1/4 cup heavy cream
2 cups (4 sticks) butter, chilled,
 chopped

■ *Makes about 2¹/2 cups*

Cook the hot sauce in a saucepot over medium-high heat until reduced to a syrupy consistency, whisking constantly to avoid burning. Whisk in the cream and reduce the heat to low. Add the butter a few pieces at a time, whisking constantly to incorporate completely after each addition. Cook until completely smooth, whisking constantly to keep the mixture from breaking.

LEMON BEURRE BLANC

INGREDIENTS

1 lemon, peeled
1/2 shallot, chopped
1 bay leaf
2 black peppercorns
1/4 cup white wine
1/4 cup heavy whipping cream
1 cup (2 sticks) butter, chilled,
 chopped
kosher salt and white pepper to taste

■ *Makes about 1 cup*

Combine the lemon, shallot, bay leaf, peppercorns and wine in a medium saucepan and cook over medium-high heat until reduced by 1/2. Whisk in the heavy cream and cook until thickened, stirring occasionally.

Reduce the heat to low and add the butter a few pieces at a time, whisking constantly to incorporate well after each addition; the sauce will break if the butter is added too quickly. Season with kosher salt and white pepper. Remove from the heat and pour through a fine strainer into a clean container.

We always keep both Crystal and Tabasco brand hot sauces on hand in the kitchen at Palace Café and at home. Both are excellent locally produced products with unique, but different, flavors, because they're each made with different peppers. We like Crystal in our fish dishes, but prefer Tabasco in our gumbo. Experiment and use what tastes best to you in a particular dish.

BRINE

INGREDIENTS

1 onion, finely chopped
4 bay leaves
8 black peppercorns
1 teaspoon crushed red pepper
2 tablespoons chopped fresh
    rosemary
2 tablespoons chopped fresh thyme
1/2 cup molasses
1/2 cup soy sauce
1/4 cup kosher salt
6 cups water
6 cups ice

■ *Makes enough to brine 2 chickens,*
2 rabbits, or 20 pork chops

Combine the onion, bay leaves, peppercorns, red pepper, rosemary, thyme, molasses, soy sauce, kosher salt and water in a large stockpot and bring to a boil. Reduce the heat and simmer for 10 minutes. Remove from the heat and let stand for 5 to 10 minutes. Add the ice and let stand until melted.

Soak meat to be smoked in the brine for 24 hours. Brining will enhance the natural flavors and keep it moist and juicy.

CRAB STOCK

INGREDIENTS

5 pounds gumbo crabs
1 cup finely chopped onion
1 cup finely chopped celery
1 cup finely chopped carrot
1 cup sliced leeks
6 bay leaves
1/4 cup chopped fresh thyme
1/4 cup chopped fresh tarragon
8 peppercorns
stems of 1 bunch parsley
1 orange, peeled
1 lemon, peeled
1 cup white wine
1 gallon (16 cups) cold water

■ *Makes about 3/4 gallon, or*
about 12 cups

Preheat the oven to 350 degrees. Place the crabs in a large roasting pan. Roast the crabs until they are bright orange. Remove the crabs to a large stockpot. Add a small amount of water to the roasting pan and stir to deglaze the pan. Add the liquid to the stockpot.

Add the onion, celery, carrot, leeks, bay leaves, thyme, tarragon, peppercorns, parsley stems, orange and lemon to the stockpot. Stir in the wine and cold water. Bring to a boil and reduce the heat. Simmer for 1 to 1 1/2 hours, skimming the surface as necessary. Strain through a fine strainer into a clean container or ice cube trays. Store in the refrigerator or freeze until needed.

Stocks are time consuming, but well worth the effort. They make all the difference in your soups and sauces and are one key reason why restaurant cooking tastes so great. Just put some stock on to cook when you have the time. When it's finished cooking, freeze it in ice-cube trays for easy pre-measured use later.

CHICKEN STOCK

INGREDIENTS

bones of 4 chickens, about
    4 pounds bones
2 cups finely chopped onions
1 cup finely chopped celery
1 cup finely chopped carrot
6 bay leaves
1/4 cup chopped fresh thyme
8 black peppercorns
1 gallon (16 cups) cold water
1 cup white wine (optional)

■ *Makes about 3/4 gallon, or
about 12 cups*

Rinse the chicken bones well and combine with the onions, celery and carrot in a large stockpot. Add the bay leaves, thyme, peppercorns, water and wine.

Bring to a boil and reduce the heat. Simmer for 6 to 8 hours, skimming the surface as necessary. Strain through a fine strainer into a clean container or ice cube trays. Store in the refrigerator or freeze until needed.

DUCK STOCK

INGREDIENTS

carcasses of 2 or 3 (4- to 5-pound)
    ducks
2 cups finely chopped onions
1 cup finely chopped celery
1 cup finely chopped carrot
6 bay leaves
4 sprigs of rosemary
8 black peppercorns
1 1/2 gallons (24 cups) cold water

■ *Makes about 1 gallon, or
about 16 cups*

Preheat the oven to 350 degrees. Rinse the duck bones well and cut each carcass into 2 or 3 pieces. Place in a roasting pan. Roast for 20 minutes or until golden brown. Cool to room temperature.

Combine the roasted duck bones with the onions, celery, carrot, bay leaves, rosemary, peppercorns and cold water in a large stockpot. Bring to a boil and reduce the heat. Simmer for 6 to 8 hours, skimming the surface as necessary. Strain through a fine strainer into a clean container or ice cube trays. Store in the refrigerator or freeze until needed.

Always start stocks with cold water and bring the water temperature up gradually to maximize the flavor. And, always simmer stocks rather than boiling them. Boiling cooks the fat back into the stock and results in a cloudy, oily stock.

VEAL STOCK

INGREDIENTS

5 pounds veal bones
3 to 5 pounds beef scraps, coarsely
    chopped
4 cups red wine
2 cups finely chopped onions
1 cup finely chopped celery
1 cup finely chopped carrot
6 bay leaves
1/4 cup chopped fresh thyme
1/4 cup chopped fresh oregano
1/4 cup chopped fresh basil
8 black peppercorns
1/2 cup tomato paste
1 1/2 gallons (24 cups) cold water

■ *Makes about 2 gallons, or
about 32 cups*

Preheat the oven to 350 degrees. Rinse the veal bones well and combine with the beef scraps in a roasting pan. Roast for 25 minutes or until the bones are golden brown and the beef scraps are brown. Remove the bones and beef to a large stockpot. Add the wine to the roasting pan and stir to deglaze the pan. Add the liquid to the stockpot.

Add the onions, celery, carrot, bay leaves, thyme, oregano, basil, peppercorns and tomato paste and mix well. Cook over medium heat for 10 minutes. Add the cold water and bring to a boil. Reduce the heat and simmer for 12 to 24 hours, skimming the surface as necessary. Strain through a fine strainer into a clean container or ice cube trays. Store in the refrigerator or freeze until needed.

FISH STOCK

INGREDIENTS

5 pounds fish bones, heads removed
1 cup finely chopped onion
1 cup finely chopped celery
1 cup finely chopped carrot
1 cup sliced leeks
6 bay leaves
1/4 cup chopped fresh thyme
1/4 cup chopped fresh tarragon
stems of 1 bunch parsley, chopped
8 peppercorns
1 cup white wine
1 gallon (16 cups) cold water

■ *Makes about 3/4 gallon, or
about 12 cups*

Rinse the fish bones well and combine with the onion, celery, carrot, leeks, bay leaves, thyme, tarragon, parsley stems and peppercorns in a large stockpot. Add the wine and cold water. Bring to a boil and reduce the heat. Simmer for 1 to 1 1/2 hours, skimming the surface as necessary. Strain through a fine strainer into a clean container or ice cube trays. Store in the refrigerator or freeze until needed.

You can substitute dried herbs for fresh herbs in stocks. As a general rule of thumb, one teaspoon of dried herbs can be substituted for one tablespoon of fresh herbs.

RED WINE DEMI-GLACE

INGREDIENTS

2 cups finely chopped onions
1 cup finely chopped celery
1 cup finely chopped carrot
2 bay leaves
1 tablespoon black peppercorns
2 cups red wine
4 gallons veal stock (page 199)
2 sprigs of fresh thyme

■ *Makes 1/2 gallon, or 8 cups*

Combine the onions, celery and carrot in a 5-gallon stockpot. Cook over high heat until the vegetables are caramelized. Add the bay leaves, peppercorns and wine, stirring to deglaze the stockpot. Cook until the liquid is reduced by 1/2.

Stir in the veal stock. Simmer for 2 1/2 to 3 hours or until the mixture is reduced to about 8 cups of demi-glace with the consistency of molasses, adding the thyme sprigs during the last 30 minutes of cooking time; skim the surface as necessary. Strain through a fine strainer into a storage container.

VEAL DEMI-GLACE

INGREDIENTS

5 pounds veal bones
3 to 5 pounds beef scraps
4 cups red wine
2 cups finely chopped onions
1 cup finely chopped celery
1 cup finely chopped carrot
6 bay leaves
1/4 cup chopped fresh thyme
1/4 cup chopped fresh oregano
1/4 cup chopped fresh basil
8 peppercorns
1/2 cup tomato paste
3 gallons veal stock (page 199)

■ *Makes about 1/2 gallon, or about 8 cups*

Preheat the oven to 350 degrees. Rinse the veal bones well and place in a roasting pan. Roast until golden brown. Brown the beef scraps in a large stockpot. Add the veal bones to the stockpot. Add the wine to the roasting pan and stir to deglaze the pan. Stir the liquid into the stockpot.

Add the onions, celery, carrot, bay leaves, thyme, oregano, basil, peppercorns and tomato paste and mix well. Cook over medium heat for 10 minutes.

Add the veal stock and bring to a boil. Reduce the heat and simmer for 2 1/2 to 3 hours or until the mixture has the consistency of molasses, skimming the surface as necessary. Strain through a fine strainer into a storage container.

Demi-glaces are even more time consuming to make than stocks, but they are easy to make and well worth the time and ambition. Don't rule out a recipe just because it calls for a demi-glace, however. Even if you don't have time to make it yourself, a lot of specialty food stores and better grocery stores carry demi-glaces.

SHRIMP BOIL

INGREDIENTS

2 medium onions, coarsely chopped
1 bunch celery, coarsely chopped
4 carrots, peeled, coarsely chopped
2 gallons water
1 cup Crystal hot sauce
1/2 cup cayenne pepper
1/4 cup black peppercorns
6 bay leaves
1/2 cup salt
3 (3-ounce) packages Zatarain's
    crab boil
3 lemons, cut into halves

■ *Makes enough to cook 5 pounds of shrimp*

Combine the onions, celery and carrots with the water in a large stockpot. Add the pepper sauce, cayenne pepper, peppercorns, bay leaves, salt, crab boil and lemons and bring to a boil.

To cook 5 pounds of shrimp, add the shrimp to the stockpot and turn off the heat. Let stand for 10 to 12 minutes then remove the shrimp with a slotted spoon.

CREOLE SEASONING

INGREDIENTS

1/2 cup salt
1/4 cup granulated garlic
1/4 cup granulated onion
2 tablespoons paprika
4 teaspoons cayenne pepper
1 teaspoon black pepper

■ *Makes 1¹/4 cups*

Combine the salt, granulated garlic, granulated onion, paprika, cayenne pepper and black pepper in a small bowl and mix well. Spoon into an airtight storage container.

As Creole and Cajun cooking has become more and more popular around the world, a lot of great Creole seasoning blends have hit the market. Some include dried herbs and a number of other ingredients. In our restaurants, we use a well-balanced blend of six simple ingredients that enhance and add flavor without overpowering the dish. Use this blend whenever a recipe calls for Creole seasoning.

SOURCES

Abita Brewing Co., L.L.C.
P.O. Box 762
Abita Springs, LA 70420
800-737-2311
www.abita.com
*For Abita® Amber beer and other great
Louisiana beers*

Baumer Foods, Inc.
4301 Tulane Avenue
New Orleans, LA 70119
504-561-0392
For Crystal® Hot Sauce (nationally distributed)

Big Fisherman
3301 Magazine Street
New Orleans, LA 70115
888-567-9907
www.bigfishermanseafood.com
*For crawfish tails, Louisiana redfish, catfish
fillets, oysters in and out of the shells, jumbo
lump crabmeat, alligator, soft-shell crabs, turtle
meat, andouille, tasso, boudin, frog legs and
seafood boil*

Dean & Deluca
800-221-7714
www.deandeluca.com
*For meats, cheeses, oils, spices and other
specialty foods*

Falcon Rice Mill, Inc.
Box 771
Crowley, LA 70527
800-738-7423
www.falconrice.com
For Cajun Country brand popcorn rice

Gazin's Cajun Creole Cuisine
800-262-6410
www.gazins.com
*For Creole Country brand andouille sausage,
tasso and other Louisiana products*

Hudson Valley Foie Gras
80 Brooks Road
Ferndale, NY 12734
914-292-2500
www.hudsonvalleyfoiegras.com
*For foie gras, duck leg confit and other
duck products*

Maple Leaf Farms
www.mapleleaffarms.com
*Website features a "duck finder" that identifies
the nearest store selling Maple Leaf Farm ducks;
deboning and cooking instructions*

McIlhenny Co.
Avery Island, LA 70513
888-TABASCO
www.tabasco.com
For Tabasco® Sauce

New Orleans Fish House
921 South Dupre Street
New Orleans, LA 70125
800-839-3474
www.nofh.com
For crawfish, shrimp, oysters and fish

P&J Oyster Company
1039 Toulouse Street
New Orleans, LA 70112
504-523-2651
www.efresh.com
For Gulf oysters

Steen Syrup Mill, Inc.
P.O. Box 339
Abbeville, LA 70510
800-725-1654
www.steensyrup.com
For cane vinegar, dark and light molasses

Urbani USA
29-24 40th Avenue
Long Island City, NY 11101
800-281-2330
www.urbaniusa.com
*For truffles, truffle oil, wild mushrooms, meats
(rabbit, poussin, quail) and seafood*

Zatarain's
82 First Street
Gretna, LA 70053
504-367-2950
www.zatarain.com
For seafood boil, Creole mustard and seasonings

For additional information, contact
us at 504-521-8313 or by e-mail at
marketing@dbrennanrestaurants.com